Y0-AAU-908

ABOUT THIS NO NONSENSE

SUCCESS GUIDE™

This No Nonsense Success Guide, like each Success Guide has been designed to live up to *both* parts of its name . . . to provide you with useful No Nonsense information *and* to increase your personal chances for Success!

A new business must have sufficient money on hand before it opens its doors. This book opens the doors you will have to enter to get the money you need to get started!

It tells you what you have to do to get venture capitalists and bankers to say YES!

It shows you where you can find today's primary sources of venture capital — including NAMES, ADDRESSES & TELEPHONE NUMBERS!

It even includes all of the information which you will need to join the nation's first computer "matching" network between investors and entrepreneurs!

HOW (AND WHERE) TO GET THE MONEY TO GET STARTED is the one book you need *before* starting a business of your own!

NO NONSENSE SUCCESS GUIDES:™

NO NONSENSE

SUCCESS GUIDE™

HOW
(AND WHERE)
TO GET THE
MONEY TO GET
STARTED

STEVE KAHN

LONGMEADOW PRESS

This publication is designed to provide accurate and authoritative information with regard to the subject matter covered. It is sold with the understanding that neither the publisher nor the authors are engaged in rendering legal, accounting or other professional services regarding the subject matter covered. If legal advice or other expert assistance is desired, the services of a competent professional person should be sought.

How (And Where) To Get The Money To Get Started

Copyright © 1987 by The Keasy Corporation. All rights reserved.

Cover design by Tom Fowler, Inc.

Composition by Tod Clonan Associates, Inc.

Published by Longmeadow Press, 201 High Ridge Road, Stamford, Connecticut 06904. No part of this book may be reproduced or used in any form or by any means, electronic or mechanical, including photocopying, recording, or by an information storage and retrieval system, without permission in writing from the publisher.

No Nonsense Success Guide is a Trade Mark controlled by Longmeadow Press.

ISBN: 0-681-40127-3

Printed in the United States of America

0 9 8 7 6 5 4 3 2 1

TABLE OF CONTENTS

1

THE MONEY YOU WILL NEED TO BEGIN YOUR BUSINESS

You've got guaranteed reservations at the hotel of your choice and you're planning to drive there in your brand-new car. Nothing, it would seem, could delay or disrupt — or even prevent — you from arriving at your destination.

Unless you run out of gas along the way!

It is similar with a new business.

Even with a wonderful idea, brilliant marketing plans and a supportive group of family and friends cheering you on, your new business will most likely fail if you don't have sufficient capital to carry it through to that critical turning point: Where potential becomes profit.

Not having enough money in the bank is as dangerous as not having enough gas in the tank: In both instances, you will fall short of your goal.

That's the bad news.

This book is mostly about the good news — about the availability of capital and about what it will take for you to avail yourself of that capital.

Raising money is never an easy or even a comfortable process — whether you're trying to acquire $500 from your favorite uncle, $5000 from your neighborhood banker or $50,000 from a buttoned-down venture capitalist.

You can take comfort in the fact that some of today's most successful businesses ("household names") barely survived the money-raising process.

The only reason they survived was because of the vision and the determination of their founders — entrepreneurs who believed in themselves and in the enterprises which they were creating.

Reading this book suggests that you share these qualities.

This book is filled with practical advice and even with the names, addresses and telephone numbers of currently active venture capital providers.

Hopefully, you will be able to put this information to good use — because you *will* need to have sufficient capital on hand *before* you start your business.

Raising money for a new business is *not* an impossible task. It is, however, a time-consuming, energy-consuming and ego-consuming process.

The purpose of this book is to help you to conserve some of your time, energy and ego by providing you with a one-stop source of basic information.

Perhaps the most basic information of all — from an entrepreneur's perspective — is that there is more than one kind of money.

The 4 Categories of Money You Will Need

You are already familiar with the concept of dealing with different "kinds" of money. There is, for example, the money you spend on life's basic needs such as food, rent and clothing. Then there is the money you save — for a vacation, a first house or a child's college education. Thus, even in a simple household context, there are at least two kinds of money: "Spending" money and "saving" money.

For a new business, you will have to make provisions for at least four categories of capital.

1. Start-Up Capital

Start-up capital is the money you must have on hand to open your doors for business. It includes all of the money you will need to spend before you can reasonably expect to have any money coming into the business.

It will have to provide for such typical start-up expenses as:

- Rental security deposits — and on-going monthly rent payments.
- Telephone company deposits — and on-going monthly phone bills.
- Utility company deposits — and on-going monthly utility bills.
- Office furniture and equipment
- Legal fees
- Accounting fees
- License fees (if any)
- Payroll funds — employees will have to be paid whether or not you are able to pay yourself.
- Insurance premiums
- Stationery — including letterheads, business cards, etc.
- Advertising and/or promotion
- Reserve funds — for the unexpected expenses that *always* seem to crop up in a new business.

2. Working Capital

It can be characterized as working capital or operating capital. Both names describe its purpose.

It is the money you will need to run your business in every aspect. It is the money you will need to purchase those goods, services and materials you need to serve your customers. It is the money you will need to keep your operations functioning even when the orders aren't coming in as quickly as you anticipated.

A new business cannot afford any embarrassing interruptions caused by lack of funds. Nothing will make new or prospective customers more nervous. Sufficient working capital will prevent that — and give your new business the appearance of a functioning, thriving operation.

3. Growth Capital

Sometimes called expansion capital, these are the funds you will need to expand operations. There is a small irony here. The need for this category of capital suggests that things are going well — but, in real life, satisfied customers and abundant orders don't always translate into immediate positive cash flow, high profits or the capital needed to meet the increased needs of a growing business.

Whereas your start-up capital and working capital *have* to be in place when you begin your business, your growth capital does not have to be in place at that moment — but it should be *potentially* available from sources to whom you have ready access and to whom you have already spoken about the upside capital needs of your new business.

4. Survival Capital

Its slightly less dramatic name is "living" capital.

Start-up, working and growth capital relate to your business. Survival capital relates to *you.*

It is the money you will need to enable you to live whatever lifestyle you (and your family) need to feel comfortable while you are building a business that may not provide you with any income for a sustained period of time.

This category of money will not be provided by anyone but you. There are different formulas for how much is "enough." That is a judgment that each entrepreneur has to make for himself considering his particular circumstances. Our advice would be that you should put aside *more money than you anticipate needing under the worst-case scenario.*

A new entrepreneur will inevitably take his business problems home with him at night; however, he should never have to worry about the welfare of his home and family during business hours. Sufficient survival capital will provide that dimension of personal assurance.

You will want to have that personal assurance — and insurance — because the process of raising capital for your new business will be filled with uncertainties.

Your success in acquiring the capital you need will depend on a variety of factors, some as unpredictable as timing and luck; others directly attributable to your thoughtful preparation of material and your equally thoughtful selection of prospective investors.

This book can only help you with the preparation and selection.

There is, additionally, only one other factor of which we are entirely confident: *The identity of your first investor.*

Although he needs no introduction, we will introduce him to you in the next chapter.

2

YOUR FIRST INVESTOR

The National Federation of Independent Business reports that nearly 60% of the capital raised for new businesses is provided by the entrepreneurs themselves.

If you add the 9% of capital which the Federation estimates to be provided by the entrepreneur's friends and family, *then nearly seven out of every 10 new business investment dollars are provided either directly or indirectly by the new entrepreneur.*

Most of this book is concerned with the ability of the new entrepreneur to acquire what is often defined as *OPM — "Other People's Money."*

Yet, no matter how much OPM you manage to collect, you will almost always have to make a meaningful investment of your own.

This is because of one very basic factor: *Investors will hesitate — and, most often, refuse outright — to invest in people who won't invest in themselves.*

Your 5 Sources For Self-Investment Funds

1. Savings

Not only is this the most obvious source, it is also the only one which doesn't have to be "paid back" in the traditional sense — although you will probably want to re-build your savings once your new business is on track.

If becoming an entrepreneur has been a constant, long-term goal, and you've managed to put aside significant sums (beyond the survival capital we spoke of in the preceding chapter), then you have an equally significant head-start in your money-raising process.

It is entirely possible that, depending on the magnitude of your business, you may have been able to save all of the capital which you need. In that case, deciding to borrow additional money or raise equity capital becomes an entirely personal decision. You may want to add some OPM to your investment mix even if you don't have to.

Most likely, you will have been able to amass a sum of savings less than your total capital requirements. In this instance, the more cash you have on hand to invest, the more impressed your prospective investors and lenders will be.

In any event, savings enable you to make investment decisions without having to rely on others; you know how much money you have on hand and how much money you can invest in your new business.

Savings, therefore, are probably your most comfortable source of self-investment funds.

2. Life Insurance

If you hold a life insurance policy with built-up "cash value," the provisions of your particular policy may enable you to borrow against that value at favorable, below-market interest rates.

You will, however, want to make certain that the basic benefits of the policy will not be affected by the borrowing.

Additionally, under the *Tax Reform Act of 1986,* some or all of the interest may not be deductible on your tax return; the less interest you are permitted to deduct, the more "expensive" the cost of that borrowed money becomes. *Thus, before making any decision to borrow against the cash value of your life insurance, be certain to determine the consequences of that decision with your accountant or attorney.*

3. Home Equity

Home equity loans have become a very fashionable method of borrowing. On the surface, they appear to be uncommonly attractive, based on a wonderful premise: The value of your home has increased over the years and you've let all that additional equity sit idle. Now, you can tap into the increased value — up to whatever limits are set by the lender — simply by writing a check whenever you need additional funds.

Under certain circumstances, particularly those specifically defined by the new tax laws, home equity loans can, in fact, be reasonable sources for borrowed funds.

Under most other circumstances, they can be very dangerous — for at least two reasons. (1) They are nothing less than a second mortgage on your house. That means that, in case of default, you can run the very real risk of losing your house. (2) Under the new tax laws, some or all of the interest may not be deductible, causing you the same potential problems we noted while discussing life insurance.

We would encourage you to carefully consider the consequences of getting a home equity line of credit with your accountant and attorney before making a decision in this regard.

4. Credit Cards

Recently, a young motion picture producer received a great deal of publicity because he was able to finance his first low-budget film with his bank credit cards.

It made for a nice story, which became even better because the movie received good reviews and the young producer was able to pay off his credit card cash advances.

There are stories of other entrepreneurs who have applied for a stream of bank credit cards, seeking high limits on each of them, in anticipation of using them as the start-up capital for their new business.

Fundamentally, this is not a sound idea — partly because of the new tax laws which we have already mentioned and partly because even the best-intentioned entrepreneur can quickly fall into the trap of credit card abuse.

If you need a *small* sum of money in advance of beginning a business — say, to hire a consultant or test a product on a very modest basis — taking a small advance against your bank credit card (one which you are confident of re-paying on time no matter what the consultant or the test indicates) might be OK.

To use your credit cards for any other purpose would, quite frankly, be foolish. Bank credit cards carry high rates of interest (much of which no longer can be deducted and, in time, none of which will be deductible) and are not appropriate sources of start-up capital, in our view.

5. Friends and Family

For the purposes of this chapter, we will consider friends and family to be an extension of yourself.

Many people believe that nothing can spoil a friendship or relationship quicker than asking a friend or relative for money; others will say, "Nonsense, what are friends and relatives for?"

It is not an argument we will enter. Our only advice would be to make any arrangements with friends or relatives very business-like and to work hard at not permitting your business interests to disrupt your friendship or relationship.

The balance of this book deals with *OPM — Other People's Money.*

However, as we have indicated, you will not be in a position to solicit and receive OPM unless you are ready, willing and able to put some of your own money on the line.

Thus, as we suggested at the end of the preceding chapter, your first investor needs no introduction!

3

THE KEY TO YOUR BUSINESS PLAN: THE EXECUTIVE SUMMARY

You didn't have to educate your first investor about yourself and your business.

You *will* have to educate every other prospective investor about the unique properties and people which will constitute the heart of the business for which you are seeking their money.

The key to this education will be your Business Plan.

And the key to your business plan is the Executive Summary.

We will discuss them in reverse order — because if your prospective investors don't respond to your Executive Summary, you will not have the opportunity to present them with your complete Business Plan.

Consider The Executive Summary
A 2-Minute Drill

The most successful venture capitalists and lenders receive dozens of new business proposals each week. Some of them are short; most of them are too long.

The only way for a new entrepreneur to break through this clutter of material is with a neatly presented, succinctly written summary of his business and his financial needs. *If possible, it should be no longer than two pages.*

This is the so-called Executive Summary.

It should contain these four items:

1. A brief description of your product or service and its market potential.

2. A brief description of your management team, emphasizing its previous successes in a similar or related fields.

3. Financial summaries, projecting five years of anticipated revenues, expenses and income.

4. A direct statement of how much investment money you are asking for, and how you will apply those funds.

This Summary should be accompanied by a short covering letter offering to transmit your complete Business Plan upon request.

Whether or not your prospect eventually elects to invest in your business or not, a well-prepared Executive Summary will bring you two immediate benefits: (1) Your prospect will be grateful to you for respecting his time, and (2) you will have significantly enhanced your chances of having your Summary read.

If there is no additional interest on your prospective investor's part, you will at least have saved the cost of postage and printing associated with the transmittal of a complete Business Plan.

If you have evoked some interest, then you will have the

opportunity to tell — and sell — your complete story through the most traditional entrepreneurial marketing device: The Business Plan.

The Business Plan: Marketing For Money

There are billions of snowflakes and millions of fingerprints but, as you know from childhood, no two are ever alike.

It is the same way with business plans: A venture capitalist may receive thousands during the course of a year but no two are ever alike.

Therein lies the new entrepreneur's problem — and opportunity.

Obviously, you have to begin with a unique product or service and a strong management team. Beyond that, however, what will distinguish your Business Plan is its directness, its honesty and its completeness.

The format of the classic Business Plan is traditional:

- **The Executive Summary.** The same one we've already spoken of. If the prospect has already seen it, it will help him to make the connection with your proposal. If he's seeing it for the first time, it will serve as an introduction and preview of the entire plan.

- **Table of Contents.** In some venture capital firms, business plans are read by specialists; that is, a financial specialist will analyze the financial statements, a marketing specialist will analyze the marketing projections, etc. All prospects, however, appreciate the courtesy and convenience of a Table of Contents.

- **The Management Team.** This is a very critical section of the plan. Investors feel most comfortable with managers who have strong track records suggestive of continued future success. The individual management profiles should be strong, simple and straightforward — without unnecessary or exaggerated information. You will note that this section precedes the section describing the product or service which will form the basis of your new company. This is indicative of the importance of strong management to prospective investors.

- **Your Product or Service.** A complete description of the product or service which is the fundamental reason for the creation of your new company. Its unique properties and characteristics should be emphasized, as well as any legal protections (such as Trade Marks and Patents) which will offer investors additional assurances. Photographs, drawings or sketches, where available and appropriate, will enhance this section.

- **The Sales and Marketing Plan.** How and where you expect to market and sell your product or service; what the size of the market is (today and in the future); what share of the market you can reasonably expect to capture. This section should include a candid analysis of your competition together with your strategy for dealing with your competitors.

- **Financial Forecasts.** You will have to present at least three separate sets of projections, each covering no less than three and preferably five years: Cash flow projections, income projections and balance sheets. (The components of each are the subject of the next chapter.) You will obviously be making a series of assumptions when you calculate these projections; insofar as possible, these assumptions should be supported by as much objective data as you can reasonably provide.

- **Funding Request.** This is the main purpose of the Business Plan, and the easiest to describe: This section sets forth how much money you are asking for and how you plan to spend and allocate that money once you receive it.

- **Appendices.** This concluding section can include anything from magazine articles about management to independent surveys about the potential of the marketplace to the entire patent application for the product you will be manufacturing. If your prospective investor has come this far, this section may simply be the icing on the cake. It should, however, like all aspects of the Business Plan, be low-keyed and confident without being suspiciously immodest.

Your Business Plan is your most important communication with your prospective investors and lenders; eventually, of course, they will want to look you in the eye before committing their money to your business.

You will never reach that point if your Business Plan is unable to convey the special properties of you and your business. Thus, spend as much time as necessary on your plan and solicit the advice of trusted friends and advisors who have experience with them. *Business plans, unlike cats and small children, usually don't get a second chance!*

4

THE 4 PRIMARY COMPONENTS OF YOUR FINANCIAL FORECAST

Ultimately, business is a numbers game.

You may have a terrific personality and a one-of-a-kind product, but professional investors and lenders try not to let emotion color their business decisions. Thus, they will look beyond your personality and your product to what they consider the most important product of all: *Your bottom line. Your numbers.*

Your Business Plan, therefore, will have to include a very carefully-prepared and completely-detailed financial forecast. You should acquire the services of a skilled accountant to help you to present these numbers as professionally as possible. (In the past, small businesses could not easily engage the services of the major accounting firms, the so-called "Big 8." That, however, has changed — as we will discuss in Chapter 14.)

Your financial forecast must include these four elements:

1. Cash flow projections.

2. Income (Profit-and-Loss) projections.

3. Pro forma balance sheets.

4. Assumptions — the underlying basis of your projections.

Your financial forecast should preferably cover five years forward; in no event should it cover less than three years.

No single format is representative of all business; therefore, we will simply outline the basic components of almost all financial forecasts. You and your accountant will have to determine and prepare the appropriate format for your particular business — and Business Plan.

1. Cash Flow Projections

These projections will clearly indicate how much money a business will receive and how much money it will disburse. They will indicate for how long the company's cash flow will be negative and at what point it will become positive cash flow. (The best example of the importance investors attach to positive cash flow is spelled out on a T-shirt worn by one of the nation's most prominent venture capitalists: "Happiness is positive cash flow.")

The most basic cash flow projection must include:

> BEGINNING CASH BALANCE
> CASH RECEIPTS
>> Collection of receivables
>> Interest income
>> Total
> CASH DISBURSEMENTS
>> Accounts payable
>> Payments of other expenses
>> Income tax payments
>> Total
> ENDING CASH BALANCE

Your cash flow projection should be prepared on a monthly basis for the first year; on a quarterly basis for years two and three, and on an annual basis for years four and five.

2. Income (Profit-and-Loss) Projections

The Small Business Administration has made an interesting distinction between the Income Statement and the Pro Forma Balance Sheets. It defines the Income Statement as a "moving picture" and the Pro Forma Balance Sheet as a "still picture."

The Pro Forma Balance Sheet presents a financial picture of the business — its assets, liabilities and ownership -- on a given date, usually the end of an accounting period. The Income Statement measures costs and expenses against sales revenues over a period of time, usually within the accounting period.

The most basic income projection should include:

> SALES
> COST OF SALES
>> Material
>> Labor
>> Overhead
>> Total
> GROSS MARGIN
> OPERATING EXPENSES
>> Cost of Sales and Marketing
>> Research and Development
>> General and Administrative
>> Total
> INCOME (LOSS) FROM OPERATIONS
> INTEREST INCOME (EXPENSE)
> INCOME (LOSS) BEFORE TAXES

TAXES ON INCOME
NET INCOME (LOSS)

Your income (profit-and-loss) projection should be prepared on a monthly basis for the first year; on a quarterly basis for years two and three, and on an annual basis for years four and five.

3. Pro Forma Balance Sheets
The most basic pro forma balance sheet should include:

    ASSETS
      Current Assets
        Cash
        Accounts Receivable
        Inventory
          Total
      Fixed Assets
        Machinery and equipment
        Buildings
        Land
          Total
      TOTAL ASSETS

    LIABILITIES
      Current liabilities
        Accounts payable
        Notes payable
        Accrued liabilities
        Reserve for taxes
          Total

        Equity
                Capital stock
                Surplus (retained earnings)
                Total
                TOTAL LIABILITIES
                AND EQUITY

Your pro forma balance sheets should be prepared on a quarterly basis for the first two years, and on an annual basis thereafter.

4. Assumptions

Since, by definition, you will be preparing and presenting financial *forecasts*, you will be basing your data on projected rather than real numbers. These numbers will be drawn from a series of assumptions which you and your advisors will have to make.

Therefore, to win the confidence of the investment community, these assumptions will have to be as conservative and credible as possible.

Never make a "best-case" assumption or, for that matter, a "worst-case" assumption. Use a middle ground based on your knowledge of your industry and your knowledge of the business which you are creating.

You will have to define (and, in truth, defend) your assumptions. For this purpose, you can refer to Government statistics, information derived from the reports of public companies in your industry and from data prepared by industry trade associations. The more detailed your "back-up," the more credible your assumptions — and your entire package of financial forecasts.

There are also broad-based reference books which you can utilize while you are developing these financial forecasts.

Perhaps the most widely-used is *Industry Norms and Key Business Ratios,* which is published by Dun and Bradstreet, the well-known financial information organization.

We began this chapter with the observation that business is ultimately a numbers game.

We will close this chapter by suggesting that providing your prospective investors and lenders with complete and credible numbers will give you a significant edge in acquiring the money which you will need to play — *and win* — the new business game!

5

BANKS: THEY CAN DO MUCH MORE THAN LEND MONEY

If you want to retain complete 100% ownership of your new business while securing some capital from outside sources, you will most likely have to deal with a commercial bank.

Banks deal in a single product: Money.

And they deal with it in an equally single-minded manner: They expect you to pay it back.

The cost of borrowing money from a bank (if, in fact, you can find a bank willing to lend money to a new business) can be considerable.

However, the cost of borrowing will *not* include having to give up any equity ownership in your business.

Thus, if you are looking for debt rather than investment capital, you will have to deal with a bank.

You may think that is bad news — but, with ever greater frequency, banks are *not* averse to establishing lending relationships with new companies. This change of attitude is mostly evidenced by smaller banks (which cannot compete with the larger big city banks and have had to find new sources of revenue), but it is a trend which has spread from coast to coast and includes banks in virtually every city in America.

Chances are that you will have to personally guarantee a loan for a new business without a proven track record of its ability to repay loans. If you can live with that provision, and you have a business plan which satisfies a bank's loan committee, banks *are* today a viable source of funds for new businesses.

This is not to suggest that it will be easy to acquire a bank loan for a new business, but at least it is no longer an impossible option.

The banking business has become increasingly competitive, to the point where even the first paragraph of this chapter has to be modified in light of recent Federal legislation. Commercial banks are still the primary banking resource for business, but Savings & Loan Associations (S&Ls) now have the right to make commercial loans, as well. It is only a small part of their business, as the law presently reads, but it has added a new player to the lending game.

From the new entrepreneur's perspective, there is an even more dramatic (and useful) development in the world of banking.

This development, however, will require the entrepreneur to give up some measure of ownership of his new business.

More and more banks are actively — and aggresively — getting into the venture capital business! They are establishing venture capital subsidiaries and reaching out to new businesses in a very un-bank-like manner.

If banking were analagous to baseball, then lending money would be equivalent to a single or, at best, a double.

Venture capitalists, on the other hand, can strike out (by

losing all of their investment in a business which goes sour)
— but they also have the opportunity to hit home runs (when
the company in which they invested turns out to be Apple
Computer or Federal Express).

Loans will continue to be the bread-and-butter business
of banks, but more and more of them are entering the venture
capital business, as well.

We have listed the venture capital subsidiaries or affiliates
of ten banks — including their telephone numbers and their
key contacts to the entrepreneurial community.

10 Venture Capital Organizations Affiliated With Major Banks

1. **BT (Bankers Trust) Capital Corporation**
   280 Park Avenue, New York, NY 10017
   (212) 850-1916
   Contacts: Martha B. Cassidy, James G. Hellmuth,
   Michael E. Nugent, Noel E. Urben.

2. **BancBoston Ventures, Inc.**
   100 Federal Street, Boston, MA 02110
   (617) 434-2442
   Contacts: Diana H. Frazier, Robert M. Freedman,
   Paul F. Hogan, Cheryl L. Krane, Stephen J. O'Leary, III,
   Jeffrey W. Wilson, Charles C. Woodard.

3. **BankAmerica Capital Corporation**
   555 California Street, San Francisco, CA 94104
   (415) 622-2230
   Contact: Patrick J. Topolski

4. **Chemical (Bank) Venture Partners, L.P.**
277 Park Avenue, New York, NY 10172
(212) 310-4949
Contacts: Steven J. Gilbert, David R. Jaffe, John F.
Kirtley, Anthony E. Malkin, Areli Marina, Barry A.
Schwimmer, Jeffrey C. Walker.

5. **Citicorp Venture Capital Limited**
Citicorp Center (28th Floor), New York, NY 10043
(212) 559-1127
Contact: Peter G. Gerry

6. **Continental Illinois Venture Corporation**
231 South LaSalle Street, Chicago, IL 60697
(312) 828-8023
Contacts: Edward K. Chandler, Samuel C. Freitag,
John L. Hines, Burton E. McGillivray, Judith Bultman
Meyer, Seth L. Pierrepont, William Putze, Scott E.
Smith.

7. **First Chicago Venture Capital**
3 First National Plaza, Chicago, IL 60670
(312) 732-5400
Contacts: John A. Canning, Jr., Kent P. Dauten.

8. **Fleet (Bank) Venture Partners**
111 Westminster Street, Providence, RI 02903
(401) 278-6770
Contact: Robert M. Van Degna.

9. **Irving (Bank) Capital Corporation**
1290 Avenue of the Americas, New York, NY 10104
(212) 408-4800
Contacts: J. Andrew McWethy, Barry A. Solomon,
Stephen A. Tuttle.

10. **Security Pacific Capital Corporation**
    650 Town Center Drive, Costa Mesa, CA 92626
    (714) 556-1964
    Contacts: Dmitry Bosky, Al Brizzard, Everett Cox,
    Gregory Forrest, John Geer, Tim Hay, Brian Jones,
    Robert Lunbeck, James McGoodwin, Ed Moss, Bill
    Service.

6

GOING PUBLIC: THE MYTHS & THE REALITIES

Many entrepreneurs have been led to believe that "going public" — selling shares (ownership) of their company to investors — is a realistic money-raising option for a new company.

It is not.

Going public is an expensive, complicated and sophisticated process which changes the very nature of an organization.

On the day a company goes public, it loses every vestige of privacy. It has to report every material change in its condition to regulatory authorities; it has to file continuous financial reports (all of which are, by law, accessible to the public); it has to report the salaries and other compensation of its key officers; it no longer can keep any "secrets" from its competitors (or anyone else, for that matter).

Thus, it is understandable that even prosperous companies which have been in business for many years as private concerns are usually extremely cautious before making the decision to go public.

These companies, however, have an advantage: They have a good chance of securing a reputable underwriter (investment banking firm) which will shepherd them through the regulatory labyrinth to the ultimate completion of their IPO (Initial Public Offering).

Most — if not all — start-up companies will be denied that advantage. They will have to scramble for a second-rate (or worse) underwriter, pay enormous fees, probably net less money than they anticipated — and still have to pay the high price of being a public company by having to meet all of the regulatory obligations — expending monies and energies which could be put to more effective use towards the growth and operation of the company.

In fairness, we should pause here to note that some start-up companies have managed to raise capital by going public, and that some of them may not even have any regrets about that decision.

The greatest lure of going public, of course, is the possibility of raising significant sums of money which would otherwise be unavailable to a new company.

However, the reality is that most new companies cannot — and should not — even entertain the thought of going public.

There may come a time when the decision to go public will be a sensible, attractive and appropriate option for a successful, growing company in need of capital.

That time is *not* at the very beginning — when the very survival of the business is at stake.

Our advice, therefore, is obvious: Going public is not a realistic option for a start-up business, and the pragmatic new entrepreneur should not believe — even for a second — that it is!

7

PRIVATE PLACEMENTS

In 1933, and again in 1980, Congress created laws designed to make it easier for small businesses to raise money.

The primary beneficiary of the Securities Act of 1933 and the Small Business Investment Incentive Act of 1980 is the so-called private placement.

Private placements can be characterized as "mini-public offerings." They can only be offered to a small group of investors, most of whom have to meet high standards as so-called "accredited" or "sophisticated" investors; they cannot be widely advertised or promoted, and they usually have restrictions attached as to their immediate re-sale ability.

In return for these limitations, most of these private placement offerings are virtually exempt from the expensive and time-consuming registration process with the Securities and Exchange Commission (SEC). Depending on the securities laws ("blue sky laws") of each particular state, these SEC-exempt securities may also be exempt from state securities registration laws. However, in many states, while they are exempt from Federal (SEC) registration, they are *not* exempt from state registration.

You will need the services of an attorney familiar with securities law as well as an equally sophisticated accountant to prepare the needed documentation for a private placement. Additionally, depending on your circumstances, you may want to engage the services of an investment banking firm to help you market your private placement.

This is not a primer on securities laws, and we will not engage in an analysis of the several exemptions provided by the two Federal laws to which we referred.

We will note, however, that *Rule 504* deals with offerings of up to $500,000 and that *Rule 505* deals with offerings of up to $5,000,000. Both fall within *Regulation D* of the 1933 Securities Act.

Typically, a *Private Placement Memorandum* will be used in connection with a private placement offering. If a private placement is like a "mini-public offering," then a Private Placement Memorandum is like a "mini-public offering statement."

Whereas your private placement may be exempt from Federal registration, your offering memorandum (and any other material) is *not* exempt from Federal anti-fraud laws; therefore, your memorandum has to be entirely truthful and accurate so as not to mislead prospective investors.

If you have a small group of investors prepared to support you, a private placement may be an ideal solution for your capital needs. Be certain to rely on experienced counsel to make sure that you are in compliance with all rules and regulations of a private placement offering in your jurisdiction.

If you are in a business which is of interest to investors (often a so-called "high-tech" venture), you may be able to find a first-class investment banking firm which has such investors as clients and is prepared to market your private placement quickly and efficiently. In this instance, of course, you will have to pay a fee for its services. A typical fee for a private placement offering may be as high as 10% of the monies raised. If you are able to engage a reputable firm which is able to bring sophisticated investors into the deal, the fee will be well-earned.

This chapter has been designed simply to give you a sense of the possibility of using the private placement as a capital-raising mechanism. It is not intended as an authoritative analysis of private placements.

Private placements, when developed in association with experts familiar with their applications, can be a useful (and successful) method of securing capital for a start-up company. They are, however, sophisticated offerings designed primarily for sophisticated investors. Therefore, you will need experienced securities counsel to guide you through the private placement process.

You've seen those disclaimers on TV car commercials where drivers engage in death-defying stunts: Do not attempt these maneuvers on your own. In the world of raising money, we would apply the same disclaimer: *Do not attempt the private placement maneuver on your own.*

8

GETTING MONEY FROM GOVERNMENT AGENCIES

During the best of times, making an application to secure financing from a government agency is a cumbersome process.

During the worst of times, depending on the philosophy of the political party in power, it can become a bureaucratic nightmare designed to discourage you from gaining your objectives.

However, at virtually all times, there are many government financing programs in place — and, with sufficient knowledge, patience and fortitude, your new business may be able to take advantage of at least some of them.

The specific programs and their detailed requirements are in a constant state of change, but the agencies which administer them are permanent and the basic objectives of each agency's policies tend to remain consistent even in the face of shifting political winds.

The Small Business Administration (SBA)

The SBA's own description of its main job is remarkably direct: *"The mission of SBA, simply put, is to help people get into business and stay in business."*

Who will the SBA assist? In its own words, the SBA will "assist, counsel and champion the millions of American small businesses which are the backbone of this country's competitive free-enterprise economy."

What is a small business? The SBA "generally defines a small business as one which is independently owned and operated and is not dominant in its field. To be eligible for SBA loans and other assistance, a business must meet a size standard set by the Agency. Specific size standard information is available through any SBA office around the country."

What kind of financial assistance does the SBA offer? The SBA offers a variety of loan programs to eligible small businesses "which cannot borrow on reasonable terms from conventional lenders without government help." The largest of these loan programs is the so-called 7(a) program, which will guarantee up to 90% of a loan but no more than $500,000. A new, start-up business will be able to secure up to 75% of its financing under this program. (Existing businesses seeking expansion, rather than start-up, capital can receive 100% financing through the 7(a) program.)

Your most direct source for complete information and for the applications you will need is your local SBA field office. Another book in this *No Nonsense Success Series* — **How To Run A Business Out Of Your Home** — contains the complete list (including telephone numbers) of all SBA field offices.

You can also get in touch with SBA headquarters in Washington:

Small Business Administration
1441 L Street, NW, Washington, DC 20416
(202) 653-6822
Public Affairs Officer: Rick Utley

Small Business Innovation Research Program

One of the SBA's primary objectives has always been to "help small business obtain a fair share" of the billions of dollars which the Federal government spends annually on goods and services.

Traditionally, small businesses did not receive many research and development (R&D) contracts. *The Small Business Innovation Development Act of 1982* was designed to encourage Federal agencies to assign such projects to small businesses, as well.

Under the law, eleven government agencies must commit a portion of their R&D funds to small businesses. The SBA has been given the task of coordinating the program between the agencies and providing information to the small business community. Even a start-up business, if it has the skills required for a particular assignment, can qualify for a research grant under this program.

Your local SBA office can provide you with the details, or you may contact the SBA's Office of Innovation, Research and Technology at the address we provided in the SBA section.

Economic Development Agency (EDA)

The EDA is a part of the Department of Commerce. Its mandate is to create jobs in areas blighted by high unemployment rates or populated by people at or below the poverty level.

To achieve these objectives, the EDA administers a loan guarantee program which will guarantee up to $10,000 for each new job created by the funds which it backs.

You can get details from EDA headquarters in Washington:

Economic Development Agency
Department of Commerce
14th & Constitution Avenues, NW
Washington, DC 20230
(202) 377-5113

Veterans Administration (VA)

The VA has some loan and loan guarantee programs available to veterans. Your local VA office can provide you with information and applications, or you can get in touch with VA headquarters in Washington:

Veterans Administration
810 Vermont Avenue, NW
Washington, DC 20420
(202) 393-4120
Public Affairs Officer: Donald Jones

Export-Import Banks
of the United States (ExIm Banks)

If your new business will be involved in exporting goods or services, the ExIm Bank may have funds available to assist you. The ExIm Bank has a number of loan guarantee and credit programs, including a Small Business Credit Program. For complete, current information, call or write:

Export-Import Bank of the United States
811 Vermont Avenue, NW
Washington, DC 20571
(202) 566-8990
Public Affairs Officer: J. Russell Boner

Minority Business Development Agency (MBDA)

The MBDA was created to assist minorities in the creation of new business opportunities. For complete, current information, call or write:

Minority Business Development Agency
14th & Constitution Avenues, NW
Washington, DC 20230
(202) 377-1936
Public Affairs Officer: Hector F. deLeon

Overseas Private Investment Corporation (OPIC)

If your new business expects to do any business in developing countries, OPIC may be able to offer assistance.

Overseas Private Investment Corporation
1615 M Street, NW, Washington, DC 20527
(202) 457-7200
Public Affairs Officer: Robert Jordan

Farmers Home Administration (FmHA)

As its name suggests, this agency of the Department of Agriculture is interested in assisting farmers. It is also committed to assisting new businesses which will be located in rural areas with populations of 25,000 or less. If your new business will be situated in such an area, you should get in touch with FmHA to determine which of their programs, if any, might be available to you.

Farmers Home Administration
U.S. Department of Agriculture
14th & Independence Avenues, SW
Washington, DC 20250
(202) 447-4581
Undersecretary of Rural Development:
Frank W. Naylor, Jr.

State and Local Economic Development Agencies

As the Federal government has curtailed and even eliminated many of the programs designed to assist new and small businesses, many states have enacted legislation to fill the breach. It is very likely that your state may already have an agency with financial assistance programs for new and small businesses.

Local (city and county) governments also will often offer some assistance to new businesses which will create new jobs and new taxes in their communities.

You should check with your state and local governments to determine whether such assistance may currently be available to you.

9

SBICs: SMALL BUSINESSES ARE THEIR ONLY BUSINESS

As you know, both the private and public sectors are filled with organizations which are primarily identified by their initials. In the preceding chapter, you were introduced to such government agencies as the SBA, the EDA and the VA. Every day, we are exposed to such companies as IBM, GTE and TWA.

The four initials which we are about to introduce may become the most important letters of every new entrepreneur's alphabet!

SBIC.

Small Business Investment Company.

Until 1958, SBICs did not exist.

Since then, they have disbursed over $6 billion by making more than 70,000 loans and investments — *all of them exclusively to small businesses!*

Collectively, SBICs are probably the most consistent source of funding for new and small businesses.

That is precisely what Congress intended when it passed the *Small Business Investment Act* in 1958. In return for pledging to finance only small businesses, SBICs qualified for long-term loans from the SBA. Using these funds, other funds and their own judgment, SBICs specialize in the business of financing small business. It is a partnership which has worked remarkably well for three decades.

The same legislation which created SBICs also created MESBICs — Minority Enterprise Small Business Investment Companies. Although all SBICs will consider applications for funds from socially and economically disadvantaged entrepreneurs, MESBICs normally make all their investments in this area.

The National Association of Small Business Investment Companies (NASBIC) represents almost 400 SBICs and MESBICs, or approximately 90% of the industry's resources.

In addition to meeting applicable Federal law — since every SBIC and MESBIC is licensed by the SBA — NASBIC members also adhere to a strict Code of Ethics.

SBICs and MESBICs can only make long-term loans (with maturities of at least 5 years) or equity investments. Thus, whether they buy shares of stock or make a straight loan, they are committed to the long-term growth of the companies in which they invest. Almost all SBICs and MESBICs will offer management and financial counseling, as well.

We are publishing the complete current directory of NASBIC members. We would share two thoughts with you. (1) SBICs are more likely to make loans and investments to companies situated near their offices. Therefore, it would probably be efficient to first contact those SBICs closest to your business. (2) Each SBIC has a different investment policy, industry preference and investment limit.

A series of letters, numbers and asterisks on the last line

of each entry will provide you with that data. You will have to refer to the "Explanation of Codes" to determine that information for each listing. That line will also indicate which of the SBICs are MESBICs.

Directory of NASBIC Members

EXPLANATION OF CODES

Preferred Limit for Loans or Investments
- A — up to $100,000
- B — up to $250,000
- C — up to $500,000
- D — up to $1 million
- E — Above $1 million

Investment Policy
- * — Will consider either loans or investments
- ** — Prefers to make long-term loans
- *** — Prefers financings with the right to acquire stock interest.

Industry Preferences
1. Communications
2. Construction & Real Estate Development
3. Natural Resources
4. Hotels, Motels & Restaurants
5. Manufacturing & Processing
6. Medical & Health Services
7. Recreation & Amusements
8. Research & Technology
9. Retailing, Wholesaling & Distribution
10. Services
11. Transportation
12. Diversified

ALABAMA

First SBIC of Alabama
Mr. David C. DeLaney, Pres.
16 Midtown Park East
Mobile, AL 36606
(205) 476-0700
C ** 12

Hickory Venture Capital Corp.
J. Thomas Noojin, Pres/Chmn.
Jeffrey C. Atkinson, VP
699 Gallatin St., Ste. A-2
Huntsville, AL 35801
(205) 539-1931
E *** 12

Remington Fund, Inc., (The)
Ms. Lana Sellers, Pres.
P.O. Box 10686
Birmingham, AL 35202
(205) 326-3509

Tuskegee Capital Corp.
Mr. A.G. Bartholomew
VP/Gen. Mgr.
4453 Richardson Rd.
Montgomery, AL 36108
(205) 281-8059

ALASKA

Alaska Business Investment Corp.
Mr. James L. Cloud, VP
P.O. Box 600
Anchorage, AK 99510
(907) 278-2071
B * 12

Calista Business Investment Corp.
Mr. Nelson N. Angapak, Pres.
Mr. Matthew Nicolai, VP/Gen. Mgr.
516 Denali St.
Anchorage, AK 99501
(907) 277-0425
MESBIC B * 12

ARIZONA

FBS Venture Capital Co.
Mr. William McKee, Pres.
Mr. Stephen W. Buchanan, Inv. Ofcr.
6900 E. Camelback Rd., Ste. 452
Scottsdale, AZ 85251
(602) 941-2160
C *** 1,5,6,8

Branch Office
Norwest Growth Fund, Inc.
Mr. Robert F. Zicarelli, Chmn.
Mr. Stephen J. Schewe, Assoc.
8777 East Via de Ventura, Ste 335
Scottsdale, AZ 85258
(602) 483-8940
E *** 1,6,8,12
(Main Office in MN)

Rocky Mountain Equity Corp.
Mr. Anthony J. Nicoli, Pres.
4530 N. Central Ave., Ste. 3
Phoenix, AZ 85012
(602) 274-7558
A ** 4,7,8,10

Sun Belt Capital Corp.
Mr. Bruce Vinci, Pres.
Mr. Joseph Henske, VP
Mr. Craig C. Lindsay, Mgr.
320 N. Central Ave., Ste. 700
Phoenix, AZ 85004
(602) 253-7600
A *** 2,4,8

VNB Capital Corp.
Mr. James G. Gardner, Pres.
Mr. John Holliman, VP/Gen. Mgr.
15 E. Monroe, Suite 1200
Phoenix, AZ 85004
(602) 261-1577
D *** 1,5,6,8,11,12

ARKANSAS

Capital Management Services, Inc.
Mr. David L. Hale, Pres.
1910 N. Grant, Ste. 200
Little Rock, AR 72207
(501) 664-8613
MESBIC A * 12

First SBIC of Arkansas, Inc.
Mr. Fred C. Burns, Pres.
Worthen Bank Bldg.
200 W. Capitol Ave., Ste. 700
Little Rock, AR 72201
(501) 378-1876
A *** 12

Independence Financial
  Services, Inc.
Mr. John Freeman, Pres.
P.O. Box 3978
Batesville, AR 72503
(501) 793-4533
B * 6,9,12

Kar-Mal Venture Capital, Inc.
Ms. Amelia S. Karam, Pres.
2821 Kavanaugh Blvd.
Little Rock, AR 72205
(501) 661-0010
MESBIC B *** 9

Power Ventures, Inc.
Mr. Dorsey D. Glover, Pres.
Hwy. 270 N./P.O. Box 518
Malvern, AR 72104
(501) 332-3695
MESBIC A * 12

Worthern Finance & Inv. Inc.
Mr. Ricor de Silveira, Pres.
P.O. Box 1681
Little Rock, AR 72203
(501) 378-1082
MESBIC C ** 4,5,6,9,10,11

CALIFORNIA
Branch Office
Atalanta Investment Co., Inc.
Mr. Alan W. Livingston, Pres.
141 El Camino Dr.
Los Angeles, CA 90212
(213) 273-1730
D *** 1,2,5,6,7,8
(Main Office in NY)

Bancorp Venture Capital, Inc.
Mr. Paul R. Blair, Pres.
Mr. Ron Miracle
2082 Michelson Dr., Suite 302
Irvine, CA 92715
(714) 752-7220
E *** 12

BankAmerica Ventures, Inc.
Mr. Robert W. Gibson, Pres.
Mr. Patrick J. Topolski, VP
555 California St., #3908
42nd Floor
San Francisco, CA 94104
(415) 622-2230
D * 12

Bay Venture Group
Mr. William R. Chandler, Gen. Ptnr.
One Embarcadero Ctr., Ste. 3303
San Francisco, CA 94111
(415) 989-7680
B *** 1,5,6,8

Brentwood Associates
Mrs. Leslie R. Shaw
VP Fin. & Admin.
11661 San Vicente Blvd., Ste. 707
Los Angeles, CA 90049
(213) 826-6581
E *** 1,12

Business Equity & Dev. Corp.
Mr. Ricardo J. Olivarez, Pres.
1411 W. Olympic Blvd., Ste. 200
Los Angeles, CA 90015
(213) 385-0351
MESBIC B * 1,5,12

CFB Venture Capital Corp.
Mr. Richard J. Roncaglia, VP.
530 B St., 2nd Fl.
San Diego, CA 92101
(619) 230-3304
B *** 1,5,6,8

CIN Investment Co.
Mr. Robert C. Weeks, Pres.
545 Middlefield Rd., #160
Menlo Park, CA 94025
(415) 328-4401
D *** 1,8

California Capital Investors, Ltd.
Mr. Arthur Bernstein, Gen. Ptnr.
Ms. Lynda Gibson, Off. Admin.
11812 San Vicente Blvd.
Los Angeles, CA 90049
(213) 820-7222
C *** 1,5,6,10,11,12

California Partners
Mr. Tim Draper, VP/CFO
3000 Sand Hill Rd.
Bldg. 4, Ste. 210
Menlo Park, CA 94025
(415) 854-7472
C *** 1,5,6,8

Camden Investments, Inc.
Mr. Edward G. Victor, Pres.
Mr. Craig M. Cogut, Counsel
Ms. Carolyn Zwirn, Asst. Sec.
9560 Wilshire Blvd., #310
Beverly Hills, CA 90212
(213) 859-9738
C *** 12

Charterway Investment Corp.
Mr. Harold Ghuang, Pres.
222 S. Hill St., Ste. 800
Los Angeles, CA 90012
(213) 687-8534
MESBIC B *** 2,4,5,7,9

Branch Office
Citicorp Venture Capital, Ltd.
Mr. J. Matthew Mackowski, VP
One Sansome St., Ste. 2410
San Francisco, CA 94104
(415) 627-6472
E *** 1,5,6,8,11
(Main Office in NY)

Branch Office
Citicorp Venture Capital, Ltd.
Mr. David A. Wegmann, VP
2200 Geng Rd., Ste. 203
Palo Alto, CA 94303
(415) 424-8000
E *** 1,5,6,8,11
(Main Office in NY)

Cogeneration Capital Fund
Mr. Howard Cann, Mng. Gen. Ptnr.
Jonathan S. Saiger, Gen. Ptnr.
300 Tamal Plaza, Ste. 190
Corte Madera, CA 94925
(415) 924-3525
D * 8

Continental Investors, Inc.
Mr. Lac Thantrong, Pres.
8781 Seaspray Dr.
Huntington Beach, CA 92646
(714) 964-5207
MESBIC B ** 4,6,9,10,12

Crocker Ventures, Inc.
Mr. Ray McDonough
One Montgomery St.
San Francisco, CA 94104
(415) 983-3636
A * 12

Crosspoint Investment Corp.
Mr. Max S. Simpson, Pres
1951 Landings Dr.
Mountain View, CA 94043
(415) 964-3545
B *** 1,5,8

Dime Investment Corp.
Mr. Chun Y. Lee, Pres.
2772 W. 8th St.
Los Angeles, CA 90005
(213) 739-1847
MESBIC A * 5,8,9,12

Enterprise Venture Cap. Corp.
Mr. Ernest de la Ossa, Pres.
Mr. Douglas S. Milroy, Op. Mgr.
1922 The Alameda, Ste. 306
San Jose, CA 95126
(408) 249-3507
B * 1,5,8

First American Cap. Funding, Inc.
Dr. Luu Trankiem, Pres.
9872 Chapman Ave., #216
Garden Grove, CA 92641
(714) 638-7171
MESBIC B * 12

First SBIC of California
Mr. Timothy Hay, Pres.
Mr. John Geer, Mng. Ptnr.
Mr. Brian Jones, Mng. Ptnr.
Mr. James McGoodwin, Mng. Ptnr.
Mr. Everett Cox, Mng. Ptnr.
Mr. Dmitry Bosky, Mng. Ptnr.
650 Town Center Drive, 17th Fl.
Costa Mesa, CA 92626
(714) 556-1964
E *** 12

Branch Office
First SBIC of California
Mr. John D. Padgett, Mng. Ptnr.
Mr. Tony Stevens, Mng. Ptnr.
155 N. Lake Ave., Suite 1010
Pasadena, CA 91109
(818) 304-3451
E *** 12

Branch Office
First SBIC of California
Mr. James B. McElwee, Mng. Ptnr.
5 Palo Alto Square, Suite 938
Palo Alto, CA 94304
(415) 424-8011
E *** 12

Hamco Capital Corp.
Mr. William R. Hambrecht, Pres.
Ms. Colleen E. Curry, VP/Sec.
One Post St., 4th Fl.
San Francisco, CA 94104
(415) 393-9813
C * 1,5,6,8

Branch Office
(Bohlen Capital Corp.)
Harvest Ventures, Inc.
Mr. Harvey J. Wertheim, Pres.
Bldg. SW3, 10080 N. Wolfe Rd.
Suite 365
Cupertino, CA 95014
D * 1,3,5,6,8
(Main Office in NY)

InterVen Partners
Mr. David B. Jones, Pres.
Mr. Jonathan E. Funk, VP
Mr. Kenneth M. Deemer, VP
Mr. Keith R. Larson, VP
445 S. Figueroa, Ste. 2940
Los Angeles, CA 90071
(213) 622-1922
E *** 1,6,8,12

Ivanhoe Venture Capital, Ltd.
Mr. Alan Toffler, Mng. Gen. Ptnr.
Mr. P. F. Wulff, Gen. Ptnr.
737 Pearl St., Ste. 201
La Jolla, CA 92037
(619) 454-8882
B *** 1,5,6,12

JeanJoo Finance, Inc.
Mr. Frank R. Remski, Gen. Mngr.
Mr. Chul-Ho Kim, Attorney
700 So. Flower St., Suite 3305
Los Angeles, CA 90017
(213) 627-6660
MESBIC B * 12

Lasung Investment & Finance Co.
Mr. Jung Su Lee, Pres.
3600 Wilshire Blvd., Ste. 1410
Los Angeles, CA 90010
(213) 384-7548
MESBIC B ** 9,12

Latigo Capital Partners
Mr. Donald A. Peterson
Gen. Ptnr.
23410 Civic Ctr. Way, Ste. E-2
Malibu, CA 90265
(213) 456-7024
C * 1,4,5,6,7,8,9

Los Angeles Capital Corp.
Mr. Kuytae Hwang, Pres.
606 N. Larchmont Blvd., Ste. 309
Los Angeles, CA 90004
(213) 460-4646
MESBIC B * 2,4,5,12

Branch Office
MBW Management, Inc.
Doan Resources
Mr. James R. Wewersing, Mng. Dir.
350 Second St., Suite 7
Los Altos, CA 94022
(415) 941-2392
D *** 1,5,6,8
(Main Office in MI)

MCA New Ventures, Inc.
Mr. W. Roderick Hamilton, Pres.
100 Universal City Plaza
Universal City, CA 91608
(818) 777-2937
MESBIC B *** 1,5,7

Merrill, Pickard, Anderson
  & Eyre I
Mr. Steven L. Merrill, Mng. Ptnr.
Two Palo Alto Sq., Ste. 425
Palo Alto, CA 94306
(415) 856-8880
E *** 1,6,8

Myriad Capital, Inc.
Mr. Chuang-I Lin, Pres.
2225 W. Commonwealth Ave., #111
Alhambra, CA 91801
(818) 289-5689
MESBIC B * 1,2,5,8,9,10,11

Branch Office
Nelson Capital Corp.
Mr. Norman Tulchin, Chmn.
10000 Santa Monica Blvd.
Los Angeles, CA 90067
(213) 556-1944
E * 12
(Main Office in NY)

New Kukje Investment Co.
Mr. C.K. Noh, Pres.
958 S. Vermont Ave., #C
Los Angeles, CA 90006
(213) 389-8679
MESBIC B * 12

New West Ventures
Mr. Tim Haidinger, Pres.
4350 Executive Dr., #206
San Diego, CA 92121
(619) 457-0722
E *** 1,4,5,6,9,10,11

Branch Office
New West Ventures
4600 Campus Dr., #103
Newport Beach, CA 92660
E *** 1,5,6,9,10,11,12

Branch Office
Orange Nassau Capital Corp.
Mr. John W. Blackburn, VP
Westerly Place
1500 Quail St., Ste. 540
Newport Beach, CA 92660
(714) 752-7811
C ** 12
(Main Office in MA)

Opportunity Capital Corp.
Mr. J. Peter Thompson, Pres.
50 California St., Ste. 2505
San Francisco, CA 94111
(415) 421-5935
MESBIC B *** 1,5,11,12

PBC Venture Capital, Inc.
Mr. Henry Wheel
Pres./Gen. Mgr.
P.O. Box 6008
Bakersfield, CA 93386
(805) 395-3206
A *** 2,5,6,8,9,12

PCF Venture Capital Corp.
Mr. Eduardo B. Cu-Unjieg, Pres.
Ms. Gina M. Guerrero, Inv. Off.
675 Mariner's Island, Blvd., #103
San Mateo, CA 94404
(415) 574-4747
B * 12

San Joaquin Capital Corp.
Mr. Chester W. Troudy, Pres.
1675 Chester Ave., Ste. 330
P.O. Box 2538
Bakersfield, CA 93303
(805) 323-7581
D *** 2,5,7,12

San Jose SBIC, Inc.
Mr. Robert T. Murphy, Pres.
100 Park Ctr. Pl., Ste. 427
San Jose, CA 95113
(408) 293-8052
C * 1,6,12

Seaport Ventures, Inc.
Mr. Michael Stolper, Pres.
Ms. Carole Rhoades, VP
525 B St., Ste. 630
San Diego, CA 92101
(619) 232-4069
B *** 12

Union Venture Corp.
Mr. Brent T. Rider, Pres.
Mr. Christopher L. Rafferty, VP
Mr. Jeffrey Watts, Sr., Inv. Off.
Mr. Thomas H. Peterson, Inv. Off.
225 S. Lake Ave., #601
Pasadena, CA 91101
(818) 304-1989
D *** 1,5,6,8

Branch Office
Union Venture Corp.
Mr. John W. Ulrich, VP
Mr. Lee R. McCracker, Inv. Ofcr.
18300 Von Karman
Irvine, CA 92713
(714) 553-7130
D *** 1,5,6,8

Unity Capital Corp.
Mr. Frank W. Owen, Pres.
4343 Morena Blvd., #3-A
San Diego, CA 92117
(619) 275-6030
MESBIC A ** 5, 12

VK Capital Co.
Mr. Franklin Van Kasper
Gen. Ptnr.
50 California St., #2350
San Francisco, CA 94111
(415) 391-5600
A * 12

Westamco Investment Co.
Mr. Leonard G. Muskin, Pres.
Mr. Scott T. Van Every, VP
8929 Wilshire Blvd., Ste. 400
Beverly Hills, CA 90211
(213) 652-8288
C * 12

Wilshire Capital Inc.
Mr. Kyn Han Lee, Pres.
3932 Wilshire Blvd., Ste. 305
Los Angeles, CA 90010
(213) 388-1314
MESBIC A ** 12

Branch Office
Wood River Capital Corp.
Mr. Peter C. Wendell, VP
3000 Sand Hill Rd., Ste. 280
Menlo Park, CA 94025
(415) 854-1000
D *** 1,5,6,10,12
(Main Office in NY)

Branch Office
Worthen Finance & Inv. Inc.
Mr. Ellis Chane, Mgr.
3660 Wilshire Blvd.
Los Angeles, CA 90010
(213) 480-1908
MESBIC D ** 12
(Main Office in AR)

Yosemite Capital Investment
Mr. J. Horace Hampton, Pres.
448 Fresno St.
Fresno, CA 93706
(209) 485-2431
MESBIC A *** 12

COLORADO
Colorado Growth Capital, Inc.
Mr. Nicholas Davis, Chmn./Pres.
Ms. Debra Chauez, Inv. Analyst
1600 Broadway, Ste. 2125
Denver, CO 80202
(303) 831-0205
B * 5,12

Enterprise Fin. Cap. Dev. Corp.
Mr. Robert N. Hampton, Pres.
P.O. Box 5840
Snowmass Village, CO 81615
(303) 923-4144
E * 12

Branch Office
FBS Venture Capital Company
Mr. Brian P. Johnson, VP
3000 Pearl St., #206
Boulder, CO 80301
(303) 442-6885
C *** 1,5,6,8
(Main Office in AZ)

InterMountain Ventures, Ltd.
Mr. Norman M. Dean, VP
Mr. E. E. Kuhns, Chmn.
1100 10th St., P.O. Box 1406
Greeley, Colorado 80632
(303) 356-3229
B *** 12

Mile Hi SBIC
Mr. E. Preston Sumner, Inv. Adv.
2505 W. 16th Ave.
Denver, CO 80204
(303) 629-5339
MESBIC A *** 1,5,6,8,12

UBD Capital Inc.
Mr. Richard B. Wigton, Pres.
1700 Broadway
Denver, CO 80274
(303) 863-6329
B * 12

CONNECTICUT
Asset Capital & Management Corp.
Mr. Ralph Smith, Pres.
608 Ferry Blvd.
Stratford, CT 06497
(203) 375-0299
A ** 2

Capital Impact
Mr. Kevin S. Tierney, Pres.
Ms. Joann M. Haines, VP
Ms. Francis P. Murray, Inv. Offcr.
Mr. John Cuticelli, Jr., Sr. VP
961 Main St.
Bridgeport, CT 06601
(203) 384-5670
C * 2,5,9,10,11,12

Capital Resource Co. of CT L.P.
Mr. I. M. Fierberg, Gen. Ptnr.
Ms. Janice Romanowski, Gen. Ptnr.
699 Bloomfield Ave.
Bloomfield, CT 06022
(203) 243-1114
B ** 12

First Connecticut SBIC (The)
Mr. David Engelson, Pres.
177 State St.
Bridgeport, CT 06604
(203) 366-4726
D * 12

Marcon Capital Corp.
Mr. Martin Cohen, Chmn.
49 Riverside Ave.
Westport, CT 06880
(203) 226-6893
C *** 1,2,9,10,12

Northeastern Capital Corp.
Mr. Louis Mingione
Pres./Exec. Dir.
61 High St.
East Haven, CT 06512
(203) 469-7901
A * 12

Regional Financial Enterprise
Mr. Robert M. Williams
Gen. Ptnr.
Mr. George E. Thomassy III
Gen. Ptnr.
Mr. Howard C. Landis
Gen. Ptnr.
36 Grove St.
New Canaan, CT 06840
(203) 966-2800
E *** 1,5,6,8,9,12

SBIC of Connecticut
Mr. Kenneth F. Zarrilli, Pres.
Mr. Emanuel Zimmer, Treas.
1115 Main St., #610
Bridgeport, CT 06604
(203) 367-3282
A * 2,9,12

DISTRICT OF COLUMBIA
Allied Capital Corp.
Mr. George C. Williams, Chmn.
Mr. David Gladstone, Pre.
1625 I St., NW, Ste. 603
Washington, DC 20006
(202) 331-1112
E *** 1,5,6,9,10,12

American Security Capital Corp.
Mr. Brian K. Mercer, VP
730 15th St., NW
Washington, DC 20013
(202) 624-4843
C *** 12

Broadcast Capital, Inc.
Mr. John Oxendine, Pres.
1771 N St., N.W., #404
Washington, DC 20036
(202) 429-5393
MESBIC A *** 1

Branch Office
Continental Investors, Inc.
Mr. Lac Thantrong, Pres.
2020 K St., NW, Ste. 350
Washington, DC 20006
(202) 466-3709
MESBIC B * 4,6,9,10,12
(Main Office in CA)

D.C. Bancorp Venture Capital Co.
Mr. Allan A. Weissburg, Pres.
1801 K St., NW
Washington, DC 20006
(202) 955-6970
C *** 5,6,9,10,12

Fulcrum Venture Capital Corp.
Mr. Divakar Kamath, Pres.
Ms. Renate K. Todd, VP
2021 K St., NW, Ste. 701
Washington, DC 20006
(202) 833-9590
MESBIC C *** 1,2,5,6,11,12

Syncom Capital Corp.
Mr. Herbert P. Wilkins, Pres.
1030 15th St., NW, Ste. 203
Washington, DC 20005
(202) 293-9428
MESBIC C **** 1

Washington Finance & Inv. Corp.
Mr. Chang H. Lie, pres.
2600 Virginia Ave., NW, #515
Washington, DC 20037
(202) 338-2900
MESBIC A *** 2,4,10,12

Branch Office
Worthen Finance & Inv. Inc.
Mr. Vernon Weaver, Mgr.
2121 K St., NW, Ste. 830
Washington, DC 20037
(202) 659-9427
MESBIC C ** 4,5,6,9,10,11
(Main Office in AR)

FLORIDA
Caribank Capital Corp.
Mr. Michael E. Chaney, Pres.
Mr. Harold F. Messner, VP
Ms. Elaine E. Healy, Invst. Ofcr.
255 E. Dania Beach Blvd.
Dania, FL 33004
(305) 925-2211
B *** 1,3,6,7,8,11

FAIC Capital Corp.
Mr. Joseph N. Hardin, Jr., Pres.
2701 S. Bayshore Dr., Ste. 402
Coconut Grove, FL 33133
(305) 854-6840
B *** 12

First Tampa Capital Corp.
Mr. Thomas L. du Pont, Pres.
Mr. Larry S. Hyman
Fin. & Inv. Mgr.
501 E. Kennedy Blvd., Ste. 806
Tampa, FL 33602
(813) 221-2171
C * 12

Ideal Financial Corp.
Mr. Ectore Reynaldo, Gen. Mgr.
780 NW 42nd Ave., Ste. 304
Miami, FL 33126
(305) 442-4653
MESBIC A ** 12

J & D Capital Corp.
Mr. Jack Carmel, Pres.
12747 Biscayne Blvd.
North Miami, FL 33160
(305) 893-0303
D * 2,5,9,12

Market Capital Corp.
Mr. Ernest E. Eads, Pres.
Mr. Jay A. Musleh, VP
Mr. Billy M. Shaw, Sec/Tres.
P.O. Box 22667
Tampa, FL 33630
(813) 247-1357
B ** 9

Small Business Assistance Corp.
Mr. Charles S. Smith, Pres.
Mr. H. N. Tillman, Secretary
2612 W. 15th St.
Panama City, FL 32401
(904) 785-9577
B * 4

Southeast Venture Capital Ltd. I
Mr. Clement L. Hofman, Pres.
One Southeast Financial Ctr.
Miami, FL 33131
(305) 375-6470
D *** 1,5,6,8,12

Universal Financial Services, Inc.
Mr. Norman Zipkin, Pres.
3550 Biscayne Blvd., Ste. 702
Miami, FL 33137
(305) 538-5464
MESBIC B ** 12

Venture Opportunities Corp.
Mr. A. Fred March, Pres.
444 Brickell Ave., Ste. 650
Miami, FL 33131
(305) 358-0359
MESBIC A *** 1,5,6,9,11,12

Verde Capital Corp.
Mr. Jose Dearing, Pres.
255 Alhambra Circle, #720
Coral Gables, FL 33134
(305) 444-8938
MESBIC B * 12

GEORGIA
Mighty Capital Corp.
Mr. Gary E. Korynoski
VP/Gen. Mgr.
50 Technology Park
Atlanta, Ste. 100
Norcross, GA 30092
(404) 448-2232
A * 12

North Riverside Capital Corp.
Mr. Thomas R. Barry, Pres.
Ms. Elizabeth G. Anderson, VP
5775-D Peachtree Dunwoody Rd.
Suite #650
Atlanta, GA 30342
(404) 252-1076
D *** 12

HAWAII
Bancorp Hawaii SBIC, Inc.
Mr. Thomas T. Triggs, VP/Mgr.
P.O. Box 2900
Honolulu, HI 96846
(808) 521-6411
A *** 12

Pacific Venture Capital, Ltd.
Mr. Dexter J. Taniguchi, Pres.
1405 N. King St., Ste. 302
Honolulu, HI 96817
(808) 847-6502
MESBIC A * 12

IDAHO
First Idaho Venture Capital Corp.
Mr. Ron J. Twilegar, Pres.
Mr. Dennis J. Clark, VP
P.O. Box 1739
Boise, ID 83701
(208) 345-3460
B *** 6,12

ILLINOIS

Abbott Capital Corp.
Mr. Richard E. Lassar, Pres.
9933 Lawler Ave., Ste. 125
Skokie, IL 60077
(312) 982-0404
A *** 1,6,10

Alpha Capital Venture Partners
Mr. Andrew H. Kalnow, Mng. Ptnr.
Mr. Daniel O'Connell, Gen. Ptnr.
3 First National Pl., Ste. 1400
Chicago, IL 60602
(312) 372-1556
C * 12

Amoco Venture Capital Co.
Mr. Gordon E. Stone, Pres.
200 E. Randolph Dr.
Chicago, IL 60601
(312) 856-6523
MESBIC C *** 3,8

Business Ventures, Inc.
Mr. Milton Lefton, Pres.
20 N. Wacker Dr., Ste. 550
Chicago, IL 60606
(312) 346-1580
B *** 12

Chicago Community Ventures Inc.
Ms. Phyllis E. George, Pres.
104 S. Michigan, #215
Chicago, IL 60603
(312) 726-6084
MESBIC B *** 4,5,12

Combined Fund, Inc. (The)
Mr. E. Patric Jones, Pres.
Ms. Carolyn Sauage, Analyst
1525 E. 53rd St., #908
Chicago, IL 60615
(312) 363-0300
C * 1,12

Continental IL Venture Corp.
Mr. John L. Hines, Pres.
231 S. LaSalle St.
Chicago, IL 60697
(312) 828-8021
E *** 1,5,6,8,9,10

First Capital Corp. of Chicago
Mr. John A. Canning, Jr., Pres.
Three First National Pl.
Ste. 1330
Chicago, IL 60670-0501
(312) 732-5400
E *** 1,5,6,9

Frontenac Capital Corp.
Mr. David A.R. Dullum, Pres.
208 S. LaSalle St., #1900
Chicago, IL 60604
(312) 368-0044
E *** 12

Mesirow Venture Capital
Mr. James C. Tyree
Managing Director
Mr. William P. Sutter, Jr.
Vice President
350 N. Clark
Chicago, IL 60610
(312) 670-6000
E *** 1,2,3,4,5,6,7,8,9,10,11,12

Branch Office
Nelson Capital Corp.
Mr. Irwin B. Nelson, Pres.
2340 Des Plaines Ave.
Des Plaines, IL 60018
(312) 296-2280
E * 12
(Main Office in NY)

Northern Capital Corp.
Mr. Robert L. Underwood, Pres.
50 S. LaSalle St.
Chicago, IL 60675
(312) 444-5399
D *** 12

Tower Ventures, Inc.
Mr. Robert T. Smith, Pres.
Sears Tower, BSC 43-50
Chicago, IL 60684
(312) 875-0571
MESBIC B *** 12

Walnut Capital Corp.
Mr. Burton W. Kanter, Chmn.
Mr. David L. Bogetz, VP
Three First National Plaza
Chicago, IL 60602
(312) 269-1732
C * 1,5,6,8

INDIANA
Circle Ventures, Inc.
Mr. Samuel Sutphin II, VP
20 N. Meridan St., 3rd Flr.
Indianapolis, IN 46240
(317) 636-7242
A *** 12

Equity Resource Co., Inc.
Mr. Michael J. Hammes, VP/Sec.
202 S. Michigan St.
South Bend, IN 46601
(219) 237-5255
B *** 5,12

1st Source Capital Corp.
Mr. Christopher Murphy, III, Pres.
Mr. Eugene L. Cavanaugh, Jr., VP
100 N. Michigan
South Bend, IN 46601
(219) 236-2180
B *** 1,3,5,6,7,8,9,11

White River Capital Corp.
Mr. David J. Blair, Pres.
Mr. Thomas D. Washburn, Vice-Chmn.
500 Washington St., P.O. Box 929
Columbus, IN 47202
(812) 376-1759
B *** 1,5,9,10,12

IOWA
MorAmerica Capital Corp.
Mr. Donald E. Flynn, Exec. VP
Mr. David R. Schroder, VP
300 American Bldg.
Cedar Rapids, IA 52401
(319) 363-8249
D *** 12

KANSAS
Kansas Venture Capital, Inc.
Mr. Larry High, VP
One Townsite Plaza
1030 First Nat'l Bank Towers
Topeka, KS 66603
(913) 233-1368
A * 5

KENTUCKY
Equal Opportunity Finance, Inc.
Mr. Frank Justice, Pres.
Mr. David Sattich, Mgr.
Mr. Donald L. Davis, Asst. Mgr.
420 Hurstbourne Ln., Ste. 201
Louisville, KY 40222
(502) 423-1943
MESBIC B *12

Financial Opportunities, Inc.
Mr. Gary F. Duerr, Gen. Mgr.
833 Starks Bldg.
Louisville, KY 40202
(502) 584-8259
A * 9

Mountain Ventures, Inc.
Mr. L. Raymond Moncrief, Pres.
911 N. Main St.
P.O. Box 628
London, KY 40741
(606) 864-5175
C * 1,5,6,10

LOUISIANA
Commercial Capital, Inc.
Mr. Milton Coxe, Acting Pres.
Mr. Michael D. Whitney, Treas.
Mr. Lou Braddock, Sec.
P.O. Box 1776
Covington, LA 70434-1776
(504) 345-8820
A * 12

Dixie Business Inv. Co., Inc.
Mr. L. Wayne Baker, Pres.
Ms. Evelyn S. Bolding, Asst. Mgr.
P.O. Box 588
Lake Providence, LA 71254
(318) 559-1558
A ** 9,10,12

First Southern Capital Corp.
Mr. Charlest Thibaut, Chmn./CEO
Ms. Carol S. Perrin, Inv. Ofcr.
P.O. Box 14418
Baton Rouge, LA 70898
(504) 769-3004
D *** 12

Louisiana Equity Capital Corp.
Mr. Melvin L. Rambin, Pres.
Mr. Jack McDonald, Inv. Ofcr.
Mr. Tom J. Adomek, Inv. Analyst
Louisiana Nat'l Bank-P.O. Box 1511
Baton Rouge, LA 70821
(504) 389-4421
C *** 1,5,6,12

Walnut Street Capital Co.
Mr. William D. Humphries
Mng. Gen. Ptnr.
231 Carondelet St., #702
New Orleans, LA 70130
(504) 525-2112
B *** 12

MAINE
Maine Capital Corp.
Mr. David M. Colt, Pres.
70 Center St.
Portland, ME 04101
(207) 772-1001
A *** 12

MARYLAND
First Maryland Capital, Inc.
Mr. Joseph Kenary, Pres.
107 W. Jefferson St.
Rockville, MD 20850
(301) 251-6630
A *** 12

Greater Washington Investors, Inc.
Mr. Don A. Christensen, Pres.
Mr. Martin S. Pinson, Sr. VP
Mr. Jeffrey T. Griffin, VP
Mr. Cyril W. Draffin, Jr., VP
5454 Wisconsin Ave., Ste. 1315
Chevy Chase, MD 20815
(301) 656-0626
D *** 8,12

Suburban Capital Corp.
Mr. Henry P. Linsert, Jr., Pres.
Mr. Steve Dubin, VP
6610 Rockledge Dr.
Bethesda, MD 20817
(301) 493-7025
D *** 5,6,8,12

MASSACHUSETTS
Atlantic Energy Capital Corp.
Mr. Joost E. Tjaden, Pres.
260 Franklin St., Ste. 1501
Boston, MA 02110
(617) 451-6220
C * 1,3,5,6,8,9,10,11,12

BancBoston Ventures, Inc.
Mr. Paul F. Hogan, Pres.
Mr. Jeffrey W. Wilson, VP/Treas.
Ms. Diana H. Frazier, VP
100 Federal St.
Boston, MA 02110
(617) 434-5700
E * 1,5,6,8

Branch Office
Boston Hambro Capital Co.
Mr. Robert Sherman, VP
One Boston Pl., Ste. 723
Boston, MA 02106
(617) 722-7055
C *** 1,5,6
(Main Office in NY)

Branch Office
Churchill International
Mr. Roy G. Helsing, VP
Ms. Julie Dunbar, Mgr.
9 Riverside Rd.
Weston, MA 02193
(617) 893-6555
D *** 1,8
(Main Office in CA)

Branch Office
First SBIC of California
Mr. Michael Cronin, Mng. Ptnr.
50 Milk St., 15th Fl.
Boston, MA 02109
(617) 542-7601
E *** 12
(Main Office in CA)

Branch Office
Fleet Venture Resources, Inc.
Mr. James A. Saalfield, VP
60 State St.
Boston, MA 02100
(617) 367-6700
E *** 1,5,6,8,9,10,11,12

Branch Office
Narragansett Capital Corp.
265 Franklin St., 11th Floor
Boston, MA 02110
(Main Office RI)

New England Capital Corp.
Mr. Z. David Patterson, Exec. VP
Mr. Thomas C. Tremblay, VP
Mr. Stuart D. Pompian, VP
One Washington Mall, 7th Flr.
Boston, MA 02108
(617) 722-6400
D *** 1,5,6,8,12

New England MESBIC, Inc.
Dr. Etang Chen, Pres.
50 Kearney Rd., Ste. 3
Needham, MA 02194
(617) 449-2066
MESBIC A * 1,4,5,6,8,9,12

Orange Nassau Capital Corp.
Mr. Joost E. Tjaden, Pres.
260 Franklin St., Ste. 1501
Boston, MA 02110
(617) 451-6220
C * 1,6,9,10,11,12

TA Associates
  Advent III Capital Co.
  Advent IV Capital Co.
  Advent V Capital Co.
  Advent Atlantic Capital Co.
  Advent Industrial Capital Co.
  Chestnut Capital Corp.
  Chestnut Capital Int'l II
  Devonshire Capital Corp.
Mr. David D. Croll, Mng. Ptnr.
Mr. Richard Churchill, Gen. Ptnr.
Mr. Stephen Gormley, Gen. Ptnr.
Mr. William Collatos, Gen. Ptnr.
Mr. James F. Wade, Assoc.
45 Milk St.
Boston, MA 02109
(617) 338-0800
E *** 1

Branch Office
Transportation Capital Corp.
Mr. Jon Hirch, Asst. VP
566 Commonwealth Ave., Ste. 810
Boston, MA 02215
(617) 262-9701
B ** 11
(Main Office in NY)

UST Capital Corp.
Mr. Arthur F.F. Snyder, Chmn.
Mr. C. Walter Dick, VP
30 Court St.
Boston, MA 02108
(617) 726-7138
B * 1,5,6,8,9,12

Vadus Capital Corp.
Mr. Joost E. Tjaden, Pres.
260 Franklin St., Ste. 1501
Boston, MA 02110
(617) 451-6220
C * 1,6,9,10,11,12

Worcester Capital Corp.
Mr. Kenneth Kidd, VP/Mgr.
446 Main St.
Worcester, MA 01608
(617) 793-4508
A *** 1,6,8

MICHIGAN
Comerica Capital Corp.
Mr. John D. Berkaw, Pres.
30150 Telegraph Rd., Ste. 245
Birmingham, MI 48010
(313) 258-5800
D * 1,5,6,8,12

Doan Resources L.P.
Mr. Ian R.N. Bund, Gen. Ptnr.
2000 Hogback Rd., Suite 2
Ann Arbor, MI 48105
(313) 971-3100
D *** 1,5,6,8

Metro-Detroit Investment Co.
Mr. William J. Fowler, Pres.
Mr. George Caracostas, VP
30777 Northwestern Hwy., Ste. 300
Farmington Hills, MI 48018
(313) 851-6300
MESBIC B * 5,6,9

Michigan Cap. & Service, Inc.
Ms. Mary L. Campbell, VP
500 First Nat'l Bldg.
201 S. Main St.
Ann Arbor, MI 48104
(313) 663-0702
D *** 1,5,6,12

Michigan Tech. Capital Corp.
Mr. Edward J. Koepel, Pres.
Technology Park, 1700 Duncan Ave.
P.O. Box 529
Hubbell, MI 49934
(906) 487-2643
B *** 3,5,8

Motor Enterprises, Inc.
Mr. James Kobus, Mgr.
3044 W. Grand Blvd., Rm. 13-152
Detroit, MI 48202
(313) 556-4273
MESBIC A ** 5

Mutual Investment Co., Inc.
Mr. Timothy J. Taylor, Treas.
21415 Civic Center Dr., Ste. 217
Southfield, MI 48076
(313) 559-5210
MESBIC B ** 9

Branch Office
Regional Financial Enterprises
Mr. Barry P. Walsh, Sr. Assoc.
Mr. James A. Parsons, Ptnr.
315 E. Eisenhower Pkwy., Ste. 300
Ann Arbor, MI 48104
(313) 769-0941
E *** 1,5,6,8,9,12
(Main Office in CT)

MINNESOTA
Control Data Capital Corp.
Mr. Doug C. Curtis, Jr., Pres.
Mr. D. R. Pickerell, Sec.
3601 W. 77th St.
Minneapolis, MN 55435
(612) 921-4118
D * 1,5,6,8

Control Data Community Ventures
  Fund, Inc.
Mr. Thomas F. Hunt, Jr., Pres.
3601 W. 77th St.
Minneapolis, MN 55435
(612) 921-4352
MESBIC C * 1,5,6,8,12

DOC Capital Co.
Mr. Jerry H. Udesen, Chmn.
603 Alworth Bldg.
Duluth, MN 55802
(218) 722-0058
A * 3,5,6,7,9,10

Branch Office
FBS Venture Capital Company
Mr. W. Ray Allen, Exec. VP
Mr. John H. Bullion, VP
7515 Wayzata Blvd., Ste. 110
Minneapolis, MN 55426
(612) 544-2754
C *** 1,5,6,8
(Main Office in AZ)

Northland Capital Corp.
Mr. George G. Barnum, Jr., Pres.
Ms. Elizabeth Barnum
Asst. Sec./Treas.
613 Missabe Bldg., 277 W. 1st St.
Duluth, MN 55802
(218) 722-0545
B *** 12

North Star Ventures, Inc.
Mr. Terrence W. Glarner, Pres.
100 S. Fifth St., #2200
Minneapolis, MN 55402
(612) 333-1133
D *** 1,5,6,8,12

North Star Venture II
Mr. Terrence W. Glarner, Pres.
100 S. Fifth St., #2200
Minneapolis, MN 55402
(612) 333-1133
D *** 1,5,6,8,12

Northwest Venture Partners
Mr. Robert F. Zicarelli, Chmn.
222 S. Ninth St., #2800
Minneapolis, MN 55402
(612) 372-8770
E *** 12

Norwest Growth Fund, Inc.
Mr. Daniel J. Haggerty, Pres.
Mr. Douglas E. Johnson, VP
Mr. Leonard J. Brandt, VP
Mr. Timothy A. Stepanek, VP
222 S. Ninth St., #2800
Minneapolis, MN 55402
(612) 372-8770
E *** 1,5,6,8,12

Retailers Growth Fund, Inc.
Mr. Cornell L. Moore, Pres.
Mr. Rick Olson, Treas.
2318 Park Ave.
Minneapolis, MN 55404
(612) 872-4929
A ** 4,9,11

Shared Ventures, Inc.
Mr. Howard Weiner, Pres.
6550 York Ave., S., Ste. 419
Minneapolis, MN 55435
(612) 925-3411
B *** 1,4,5,6,9,11

Threshold Ventures, Inc.
Mr. John L. Shannon, VP
430 Oak Grove St., Ste. 303
Minneapolis, MN 55403
(612) 874-7199
B *** 1,5,6,9,12

MISSISSIPPI
Columbia Ventures, Inc.
Mr. Maurice Reed, Chmn.
Mr. Richard P. Whitney, Pres.
P.O. Box 1066
Jackson, MS 39215
(Fully Invested)

Invest Capital Corp.
Mr. John Bise, Pres.
P.O. Box 3288
Jackson, MS 39207
(601) 969-3242
D * 12

Vicksburg SBIC
Mr. David L. May, Pres.
P.O. Box 852
Vicksburg, MS 39180
(601) 636-4762
A * 12

MISSOURI
Bankers Capital Corp.
Mr. Raymond E. Glasnapp, Pres.
Mr. Lee Glasnapp, VP
3100 Gillham Rd.
Kansas City, MO 64109
(816) 531-1600
A * 12

Capital For Business, Inc.
Mr. James B. Hebenstreit, Pres.
Mr. William O. Cannon, VP
Mr. Bart Bergman, VP
11 S. Meramec, #800
St. Louis, MO 63105
(314) 854-7427
C *** 1,5,6,8,9,10,12

Branch Office
Capital For Business, Inc.
Mr. Bart Bergman, VP
720 Main St., Suite 700
Kansas City, MO 64105
(816) 234-2357
C *** 1,5,6,8,9,10,12

Intercapco, Inc.
Mr. Thomas E. Phelps, Pres.
Mr. Mark J. Lincoln, VP
7800 Bonhomme Ave.
Clayton, MO 63105
(314) 863-0600
C *** 12

Intercapco West, Inc.
Mr. Thomas E. Phelps, Chmn.
Mr. Mark J. Lincoln, Pres.
7800 Bonhomme Ave.
Clayton, MO 63105
(314) 863-0600
C *** 12

Branch Office
MorAmerica Capital Corp.
Mr. Kevin F. Mullane, VP
Ste. 2724 - Commerce Tower Bldg.
911 Main St.
Kansas City, MO 64105
(816) 842-0114
D *** 12
(Main Office in Iowa)

United Missouri Capital Corp.
Mr. Joseph Kessinger
Exec. VP/Mgr.
928 Grand Ave., 1st Flr.
Kansas City, MO. 64106
(816) 556-7115
B * 5,6,8,10

NEW HAMPSHIRE
Granite State Capital, Inc.
Mr. Albert Hall, III, Mng. Dir.
10 Fort Eddy Rd.
Concord, NH 03301
(603) 228-9090
A * 1,5,6,10,12

Lotus Capital Corp.
Mr. Richard J. Ash, Pres.
875 Elm St.
Manchester, NH 03101
(603) 668-8617
B *** 1,6,8,12

NEW JERSEY
Capital Circulation Corp.
Ms. Judy M. Kao, Dir/Sec.
208 Main St.
Ft. Lee, NJ 07024
(201) 947-8627
MESBIC B * 12

ESLO Capital Corp.
Mr. Leo Katz, Pres.
2401 Morris Ave., Ste. 220EW
Union, NJ 07083
(201) 687-4920
B * 12

First Princeton Capital Corp.
Mr. S. Lawrence Goldstein, Pres.
227 Hamburg Tpke.
Pompton Lakes, NJ 07442
(201) 831-0330
B *** 12

Monmouth Capital Corp.
Mr. Eugene W. Landy, Pres.
Mr. Ralph B. Patterson, Exec. VP
P.O. Box 335 — 125 Wyckoff Rd.
Eatontown, NJ 07724
(201) 542-4927
C * 4,5,7,12

Branch Office
MBW Management, Inc.
   Doan Resources
Philip E. McCarthy, Mng. Dir.
365 South St., 2nd Floor
Morristown, NJ 07960
(201) 285-5533
D *** 1,5,6,8
(Main Office in MI)

Rutgers Minority Investment Co.
Mr. Oscar Figueroa, Pres.
180 University Ave., 3rd Fl.
Newark, NJ 07102
(201) 648-5627
MESBIC B *** 12

Tappan Zee Capital Corp.
Mr. Jack Birnberg, Chmn.
201 Lower Notch Rd.
Little Falls, NJ 07424
(201) 256-8280
D * 12

Unicorn Ventures, Ltd.
Mr. Frank P. Diassi, Gen. Ptnr.
Mr. Arthur B. Baer, Gen. Ptnr.
6 Commerce Dr.
Cranford, NJ 07016
(201) 276-7880
D *** 12

Unicorn Ventures II, L.P.
Mr. Frank P. Diassi, Gen. Ptnr.
Mr. Arthur B. Baer, Gen. Ptnr.
6 Commerce Dr.
Cranford, NJ 07016
(201) 276-7880
D *** 12

NEW MEXICO
Albuquerque SBIC
Mr. Albert T. Ussery, Pres.
P.O. Box 487
Albuquerque, NM 87103
(505) 247-0145
A *** 12

Associated SW Investors, Inc.
Mr. John R. Rice, Pres.
2400 Louisiana, N.E., #4
Albuquerque, NM 87110
(505) 881-0066
MESBIC B * 1,5,6,8

Equity Capital Corp.
Mr. Jerry A. Henson, Pres.
231 Washington Ave., Ste. 2
Santa Fe, NM 87501
(505) 988-4273
B *** 5,9,12

Fluid Capital Corp.
Mr. George T. Slaughter, Pres.
8421 B Montgomery Blvd., NE
Albuquerque, NM 87111
(505) 292-4747
C *** 1,2,4,5,6,12

Southwest Capital Inv. Inc.
Mr. Martin J. Roe, Pres.
3500-E Commanche Rd., NE
Albuquerque, NM 87107
(505) 884-7161
C * 12

NEW YORK
American Commercial Capital Corp.
Mr. Gerald J. Grossman, Pres.
310 Madison Ave., Ste. 1304
New York, NY 10017
(212) 986-3305
B * 2,4,5,11,12

AMEV Capital Corp.
Mr. Martin S. Orland, Pres.
One World Trade Ctr., Ste. 5001
New York, NY 10048
(201) 775-9100
D *** 1,4,5,6,9,10,11,12

Atalanta Investment Co., Inc.
Mr. L. Mark Newman, Chmn.
450 Park Ave., Ste. 2102
New York, NY 10022
(212) 832-1104
D *** 1,2,5,6,7,8

Atlantic Capital Corp.
Mr. Harald Paumgarten, Pres.
40 Wall St.
New York, NY 10005
(212) 612-0616
E *** 12

Boston Hambro Capital Co.
Mr. Edwin A. Goodman, Pres.
17 E. 71st St.
New York, NY 10021
(212) 288-7778
C *** 1,5,6

BT Capital Corp.
Mr. James G. Hellmuth, Chmn.
Mr. Noel Urben, Pres.
Mr. Keith Fox, VP
Ms. Martha Cassidy, Asst. VP
280 Park Ave.
New York, NY 10017
(212) 850-1916
E *** 5,10

The Central New York SBIC, Inc.
Mr. Albert Wertheimer, Pres.
351 S. Warren St., Ste. 600
Syracuse, NY 13202
(315) 478-5026
A *** 1,7

Chase Manhattan Capital Corp.
Mr. Gustav H. Koven, Pres.
1 Chase Manhattan Plaza
23rd, Fl.
New York, NY 10081
(212) 552-6275
E *** 1,3,5,6,7,8,10,11,12

Chemical Venture Capital Corp.
Mr. Steven J. Gilbert, Pres./CEO
Mr. Jeffrey C. Walker, VP
Mr. Michael J. Feldman, VP
277 Park Ave., 10th Fl.
New York, NY 10172
(212) 310-4949
E *** 1,4,5,6,7,8,9,10,11,12

Citicorp Venture Capital Ltd.
Mr. Peter G. Gerry, Pres.
Ms. Diane Rivas, Asst. Mgr.
153 East 53rd St., 28th Fl.
New York, NY 10043
(212) 559-1127
E *** 12

Clinton Capital Corp.
Mr. Mark Scharfman, Pres.
Mr. Alan Leavitt, VP
419 Park Ave. S.
New York, NY 10016
(212) 696-4334
E ** 12

CMNY Capital Co., Inc.
Mr. Robert Davidoff, VP
77 Water St.
New York, NY 10005
(212) 437-7078
C *** 1,5,9,10,12

College Venture Equity Corp.
Mr. Francis M. Williams, Pres.
Mr. Joseph M. Williams, VP
256 Third St., P.O. Box 135
Niagara Falls, NY 14303
(813) 248-3878
A ** 2,5,6,11,12

Croyden Capital Corp.
Mr. Victor L. Hecht, Pres.
45 Rockefeller Pl., Ste. 2165
New York, NY 10111
(212) 974-0184
B *** 12

Edwards Capital Co.
Mr. Edward Teitlebaum, Mng. Ptnr.
215 Lexington Ave., #805
New York, NY 10016
(212) 686-2568
A ** 11

Elk Associates Funding Corp.
Mr. Gary C. Granoff, Pres.
600 Third Ave., #3810
New York, NY 10016
(212) 972-8550
MESBIC B ** 11,12

Equico Capital Corp.
Mr. Duane E. Hill, Pres.
1290 Ave. of the Amer., Ste. 3400
New York, NY 10019
(212) 397-8660
MESBIC C *** 12

Everlast Capital Corp.
Mr. Frank J. Segreto, VP/CEO
350 Fifth Ave., Ste. 2805
New York, NY 10118
(212) 695-3910
MESBIC B * 2,9,10

Fairfield Equity Corp.
Mr. Matthew A. Berdon, Pres.
Mr. Samuel L. Highleyman, VP
200 E. 42nd St.
New York, NY 10017-5893
B * 1,5,7,9

Ferranti High Technology, Inc.
Mr. Sanford R. Simon, Pres.
Mr. Michael R. Simon, VP
Mr. Keith C. Laugworthy, VP Sec.
515 Madison Ave., #1225
New York, NY 10022
(212) 688-9828
D * 1,5,8,12

Fifty-Third Street Ventures, L.P.
Ms. Patricia Cloherty, Gen. Ptnr.
Mr. Daniel Tessler, Gen. Ptnr.
420 Madison Ave., #1101
New York, NY 10017
(212) 752-8010
D *** 1,5,6,8

J.H. Foster & Co., Ltd.
Mr. John H. Foster, Ptnr.
Mr. Michael J. Connelly, Exec. VP
437 Madison Ave.
New York, NY 10024
(212) 753-4810
E *** 6,10,11,12

Franklin Corp. (The)
Mr. Allen Parks, Pres.
1185 Ave. of the Americas
27th Flr.
New York, NY 10036
(212) 719-4844
E *** 5,6,8,9,11

Fundex Capital Corp.
Mr. Howard Sommer, Pres.
Mr. Martin Albert, VP
525 Northern Blvd.
Great Neck, NY 11021
(516) 466-8550
D * 12

GHW Capital Corp.
Mr. Jack Graff, Pres.
489 Fifth Ave., 2nd Fl.
New York, NY 10017
(212) 687-1708
B * 12

The Hanover Capital Corp.
Mr. John A. Selzer, VP
Mr. Stephen E. Levenson, VP
150 E. 58th St., Ste. 2710
New York, NY 10155
(212) 980-9670
B * 12

Harvest Ventures
  Asea-Harvest Partners I
  Bohlen Capital Corp.
  European Dev. Cap. Ltd.
Ptnrship.
  Noro Capital Ltd.
  767 Ltd. Ptnrshp.
  WFG-Harvest Ptnrs., Ltd.
Mr. Harvey Wertheim, Gen. Ptnr.
767 Third Ave.
New York, NY 10017
(212) 838-7776
D * 1,3,5,6,8

Ibero-American Investors Corp.
Mr. Emilio L. Serrano, Pres./CEO
Chamber of Commerce Bldg.
55 St. Paul St.
Rochester, NY 14604
(716) 262-3440
MESBIC B * 5,9,12

Intergroup Venture Capital Corp.
Mr. Ben Hauben, Pres.
230 Park Ave., Ste. 206
New York, NY 10169
(212) 661-5428
A * 12

Irving Capital Corp.
Mr. J. Andrew McWethy, Exec. VP
Mr. Barry Solomon, VP
Mr. Steve Tuttle, VP
1290 Ave. of Americas, 3rd Fl.
New York, NY 10104
(212) 408-4800
E *** 12

Key Venture Capital Corp.
Mr. John M. Lang, Pres.
Mr. Mark R. Hursty, Exec. VP/Mng.
Mr. Richard C. VanAuken, Asst. VP
60 State St.
Albany, NY 12207
(518) 447-3227
B *** 12

Kwiat Capital Corp.
Mr. Sheldon Kwiat, Pres.
Mr. Lowell Kwiat, VP/Sec.
576 Fifth Ave.
New York, NY 10036
(212) 391-2461
A ** 1,5,6,7,8,12

M & T Capital Corp.
Mr. Joseph V. Parlato, Pres.
Ms. Norma E. Gracia, Treas.
One M & T Pl., 5th Fl.
Buffalo, NY 14240
(716) 842-5881
D * 1,5,6,8,9,11,12

Madallion Funding Corp.
Mr. Alvin Murstein, Pres.
205 E. 42nd St., Ste. 2020
New York, NY 10017
(212) 682-3300
MESBIC B *** 11

Minority Equity Capital Co., Inc.
Mr. Donald Greene
Pres.
Mr. Clarence Arrington
Inv. Ofcr.
275 Madison Ave., Ste. 1901
New York, NY 10016
(212) 686-9710
MESBIC C *** 1,5,6,9,11,12

Multi-Purpose Capital Corp.
Mr. Eli B. Fine, Pres.
31 S. Broadway
Yonkers, NY 10701
(914) 963-2733
A *** 12

NatWest USA Capital Corp.
Mr. Orville G. Aarons, Sr. VP
175 Water St.
New York, NY 10038
(212) 602-1200
D * 1,3,5,6,11

Nelson Capital Corp.
Mr. Irwin B. Nelson, Pres.
591 Stewart Ave.
Garden City, NY 11530
(516) 222-2255
E * 12

Norstar Bancorp
Mr. Raymond A. Lancaster, Pres.
Mr. Joseph L. Reinhart, Analyst
Mr. Stephen Puricelli, Analyst
1450 Western Ave.
Albany, NY 12203
(518) 447-4492
D * 12

North American Funding Corp.
Mr. Franklin Wong, VP/Gen. Mgr.
177 Canal St.
New York, NY 10013
(212) 226-0080
MESBIC B * 12

North Street Capital Corp.
Mr. Ralph L. McNeal, Sr., Pres.
250 North St., RA-6S
White Plains, NY 10625
(914) 335-7901
MESBIC B *** 12

NYBDC Capital Corp.
Mr. Marshall R. Lustig, Pres.
41 State St.
Albany, NY 12207
(518) 463-2268
A * 12

Pan Pac Capital Corp.
Dr. Ing-Ping J. Lee, Pres.
19 Rector St., 35th Fl.
New York, NY 10006
(212) 344-6680
MESBIC A ** 12

Questech Capital Corp.
Dr. Earl W. Brian, Chmn.
Mr. John E. Koonce, Pres.
Ms. Barbara J. Hann, VP
600 Madison Ave.
New York, NY 10022
(212) 758-8522
D * 1,5,6,8

R & R Financial Corp.
Mr. Martin Eisenstadt, VP
1451 Broadway
New York, NY 10036
(212) 790-1400
A ** 12

Rand SBIC, Inc.
Mr. Donald A. Ross, Pres.
Mr. Thomas J. Bernard, VP
Mr. Keith B. Wiley, VP
1300 Rand Bldg.
Buffalo, NY 14203
(716) 853-0802
C *** 1,5,6,7,8,9,10,12

Peter J. Schmitt Co., Inc.
Mr. Mark A. Flint, Mgr.
P.O. Box 2
Buffalo, NY 14240
(716) 821-1400
A *** 9

Small Bus. Electronics Inv. Co.
Mr. Stanley Meisels, Pres.
1220 Peninsula Blvd.
Hewlett, NY 11557
(516) 374-0743
A * 12

Southern Tier Capital Corp.
Mr. Milton Brizel, Pres.
Mr. Harold Gold, Sec.
55 S. Main St.
Liberty, NY 12754
(914) 292-3030
A * 12

Branch Office
Tappan Zee Capital Corp.
120 N. Main St.
New City, NY 10956
(914) 634-8890
D * 12
(Main Office in NJ)

TLC Funding Corp.
Mr. Philip G. Kass, Pres.
141 S. Central Ave.
Hartsdale, NY 10530
(914) 683-1144
B ** 4,9,12

Transportation Capital Corp.
Mr. Melvin L. Hirsch, Pres.
Mr. Robert Silver, VP
Mr. Jon Hirsch, Asst. VP
Ms. Margaret Shiroky, Asst. Sec.
60 E. 42nd St., Ste. 3126
New York, NY 10165
(212) 697-4885
MESBIC B ** 11

Transworld Ventures, Ltd.
Mr. Jack H. Berger, Pres.
331 W. End Ave., Ste. 1A
New York, NY 10023
(212) 496-1010
A *** 5,10,12

Triad Capital Corp. of NY
Mr. L. Jim Barrera, Pres.
960 Southern Blvd.
Bronx, NY 10459
(212) 589-6541
MESBIC A * 1,3,6,8,9,10

Vega Capital Corp.
Mr. Victor Harz, Pres.
Mr. Ronald A. Linden, VP
720 White Plains Rd.
Scarsdale, NY 10583
(914) 472-8550
D * 12

Venture SBIC, Inc.
Mr. Arnold Feldman, Pres.
249-12 Jericho Tpke.
Floral Park, NY 11001
(516) 352-0068
A ** 2,9,12

Branch Office
Walnut Capital Corp.
Mr. Julius Goldfinger, Pres.
110 E. 59th St., 37th Floor
New York, NY 10016
(212) 750-1000
C * 1,5,6,8
(Main Office in IL)

Winfield Capital Corp.
Mr. Stanley Pechman, Pres.
237 Mamaroneck Ave.
White Plains, NY 10605
(914) 949-2600
D * 12

Wood River Capital Corp.
Ms. Elizabeth W. Smith, Pres.
645 Madison Ave.
New York, NY 10022
(212) 750-9420
D *** 1,5,6,10,12

Branch Office
Worthan Finance & Inv. Inc.
Mr. Guy Meeker, Mgr.
535 Madison Ave., 17th Fl.
New York, NY 10022
(212) 750-9100
MESBIC D ** 12
(Main Office in AR)

NORTH CAROLINA
Branch Office
Carolina Venture Capital Corp.
Mr. Thomas H. Harvey, III, Pres.
P.O. Box 646
Chapel Hill, NC 27514
B *** 1,2,4,7,11,12
(Main Office in SC)

Delta Capital, Inc.
Mr. Alex B. Wilkins, Jr., Pres.
Ms. Martha C. Kirker, Sec.
227 N. Tryon St., Ste 201
Charlotte, NC 28202
(704) 372-1410
B * 2,4,5,8,9,10

Falcon Capital Corp.
Dr. P.S. Prasad, Pres.
400 W. Fifth St.
Greenville, NC 27834
(919) 752-5918
A *** 2,4,6,9,10

Heritage Capital Corp.
Mr. Herman B. McManaway, Pres.
Mr. William R. Starnes, VP
Mr. G. Kinsey Roper, VP
2290 First Union Plaza
Charlotte, NC 28282
(704) 334-2867
C *** 12

Kitty Hawk Capital, Ltd.
Mr. Walter H. Wilkinson Jr.
Gen. Ptnr.
One Tryon Ctr., Ste. 2030
Charlotte, NC 28284
(704) 333-3777
C *** 1,5,6,8,12

NCNB SBIC Corp.
Mr. Troy McCrory, Pres.
One NCNB Plaza, TO5-2
Charlotte, NC 28255
(704) 374-5000
C * 12

NCNB Venture Corp.
Mr. Mike Elliott, Pres.
One NCNB Plaza, T39
Charlotte, NC 28255
(704) 374-0435
D *** 1,5,6,8,12

OHIO
A.T. Capital Corp.
Mr. Shailesh J. Mehta, Pres.
Mr. Robert C. Salipante, VP
900 Euclid Ave., T-18
Cleveland, OH 44101
(216) 687-4970
C * 1,6,8

Capital Funds Corp.
Mr. Carl G. Nelson, VP/Mgr.
Mr. David B. Chiloote, Asst. VP
127 Public Sq.
Cleveland, OH 44114
(216) 622-8628
C * 1,5,6,9,12

Clarion Capital Corp.
Mr. Morton Cohen
Chmn/Pres.
Mr. Michael Boeckman
VP/Chief Fin. Ofcr.
Mr. Roger W. Eaglen, VP
3555 Curtis Blvd.
Eastlake, OH 44144
(216) 953-0555
C *** 1,3,5,6,8,10,12

First Ohio Capital Corp.
Mr. Michael J. Aust, VP
606 Madison Ave.
Toledo, OH 43504
(419) 259-7146
B *** 12

Gries Investment Co.
Mr. Robert D. Gries, Pres.
Mr. Richard Brezic, VP
720 Statler Office Tower
Cleveland, OH 44115
(216) 861-1146
B *** 12

National City Capital Corp.
Mr. Michael Sherwin, Pres.
623 Euclid Ave.
Cleveland, OH 44114
(216) 575-2491
C *** 12

Branch Office
River Capital Corp.
Mr. Peter D. Van Oosterhout, Pres.
796 Huntington Bldg.
Cleveland, OH 44115
(216) 781-3655
D *** 12
(Main Office in RI)

SeaGate SBIC
Mr. Donald E. Breese, Sr. VP
245 Summit St., #1403
Toledo, OH 43603
(419) 259-8588
A *** 5,6,12

67

OKLAHOMA
Alliance Business Investment Co.
Mr. Barry M. Davis, Pres.
Mr. Mark R. Blankenship, VP
One Williams Ctr., Ste. 2000
Tulsa, OK 74172
(918) 584-3581
C *** 1,3,5,6,7,9,11,12

First OK Investment Capital Corp.
Mr. David H. Pendley, Pres.
Mr. Arthur J. Miller, VP
120 N. Robinson, Ste. 880C
Oklahoma City, OK 73102
(405) 272-4693
D *** 1,5,6,9,10,11,12

Southwest Venture Capital, Inc.
Mr. Donald J. Rubottom, Pres.
2700 E. 51st St., Ste. 340
Tulsa, OK 74105
(918) 742-3177
A *** 5,6,9,10

Western Venture Capital Corp.
Mr. William B. Baker, Pres./CEO
4900 S. Lewis
Tulsa, OK 74105
(918) 749-7981
D ** 12

OREGON
Branch Office
InterVen Partners
Mr. Wayne B. Kingsley, Chmn.
Mr. Keith L. Larson, VP
227 SW Pine St., Ste. 200
Portland, OR 97204
(503) 223-4334
E *** 1,6,8,12
(Main Office in CA)

Northern Pacific Capital Corp.
Mr. John J. Tennant, Jr., Pres.
Mr. Joseph P. Tennant, Sec.
1201 SW 12th Ave.
Portland, OR 97205
(503) 241-1255
B *** 5,9,11

Branch Office
Norwest Growth Fund, Inc.
Mr. Anthony Miadich, VP
Mr. Dale J. Vogel, VP
1300 SW Fifth Ave., Ste. 3018
Portland, OR 97201
(503) 223-6622
E *** 1,6,8,12
(Main Office in MN)

Trendwest Capital Corp.
Mr. Mark E. Nicol, Pres.
P.O. Box 5106
Klamath Fall,s OR 97601
(503) 882-8059
B *** 12

PENNSYLVANIA
Alliance Enterprise Corp.
(The Sun Company)
Mr. Terrence Hicks, VP
1801 Market St., 3rd Fl.
Philadelphia, PA 19103
(215) 977-3925
MESBIC B * 1,5

Enterprise Vent. Cap. Corp. of PA
Mr. Donald W. Cowie, VP
227 Franklin St., #215
Johnstown, PA 15901
(814) 535-7597
A * 12

Branch Office
First SBIC of California
Mr. Daniel A. Dye, Mng. Ptnr.
P.O. Box 512
Washington, PA 15301
(412) 223-0707
E *** 12
(Main Office in CA)

First Valley Capital Corp.
Mr. Matthew W. Thomas, Pres.
One Center Sq., Ste. 201
Allentown, PA 18101
(215) 776-6760
B * 12

Gtr. Phil. Ven. Cap. Corp., Inc.
Mr. Martin M. Newman, Gen. Mgr.
225 S. 15th St., Ste. 920
Philadelphia, PA 19102
(215) 732-1666
MESBIC B *** 4,5,6

Meridian Capital Corp.
Mr. Knute C. Albrecht, Pres/CEO
Mr. Jay M. Ackerman, VP
Blue Bell West, Ste. 122
Blue Bell, PA 19422
(215) 278-8907
B *** 12

PNC Capital Corp.
Mr. David M. Hillman, Exec. VP
Mr. Jeffrey H. Schultz, VP
Mr. Peter Del Presto, Inv.
Analyst
5th Ave. & Wood St., 19th Fl.
Pittsburgh, PA 15222
(412) 355-2245
C *** 1,5,6,8,9,10

PUERTO RICO
First Puerto Rico Capital, Inc.
Mr. Eliseo E. Font, Pres.
P.O. Box 816
Mayaguez, PR 00709
(809) 832-9171
MESBIC A * 12

North America Investment Corp.
Mr. S. Ruiz-Betancourt, Pres.
Banco Popular Ctr., Ste. 1710
Hato Rey, PR 00919
(809) 754-6177
MESBIC B * 5,6,9,12

RHODE ISLAND
Domestic Capital Corp.
Mr. Nathaniel B. Baker, Pres.
815 Reservoir Ave.
Cranston, RI 02910
(401) 946-3310
B * 4,5,11,12

Fleet Venture Resources, Inc.
Mr. Robert M. Van Degna, Pres.
111 Westminster St.
Providence, RI 02920
(401) 278-6770
E *** 1,5,6,8,9,10,11,12

Narragansett Capital Corp.
Mr. Arthur D. Little, Chmn.
Mr. Gregory P. Barber, VP
Mr. Roger A. Vandenberg, VP
40 Westminster St.
Providence, RI 02903
(401) 751-1000
E * 1,5,7,8,9,12

Old Stone Capital Corp.
Mr. Arthur Barton, VP
One Old Stone Sq., 11th Fl.
Providence, RI 02901
(401) 278-2559
D *** 1

River Capital Corp.
Mr. Peter D. Van Oosterhout
Pres.
Mr. Robert A. Comey, VP
Mr. Peter C. Canepa, VP
One Hospital Trust Plaza
Providence, RI 02903
(401) 278-8819
D *** 12

SOUTH CAROLINA
Carolina Venture Capital Corp.
Mr. Thomas H. Harvey III, Pres.
14 Archer Rd.
Hilton Head Island, SC 29928
(803) 842-3101
B *** 1,2,4,7,11,12

Reedy River Ventures
Mr. John M. Sterling, Gen. Ptnr.
Mr. Tee C. Hooper, Gen. Ptnr.
P.O. Box 17526
Greenville, SC 29606
(803) 297-9198
B *** 1,5,9,12

TENNESSEE
Chickasaw Capital Corp.
Mr. Thomas L. Moore, Pres.
P.O. Box 387
Memphis, TN 38147
(901) 523-6470
MESBIC D *** 2,5,6,9,10,12

Financial Resources, Inc.
Mr. Milton C. Picard, Chmn.
2800 Sterick Bldg.
Memphis, TN 38103
(901) 527-9411
B *** 1,5,6,8,10,12

Leader Capital Corp.
Mr. Edward Pruitt, Pres.
P.O. Box 708, 158 Madison Ave.
Memphis, TN 38101-0708
(901) 578-2405

Suwannee Capital Corp.
Mr. Peter R. Pettit, Pres.
Mr. Melvin Hill, VP
3030 Poplar Ave.
Memphis, TN 38111
(901) 345-4200
C ** 9

Tennessee Equity Capital Corp.
Mr. Walter S. Cohen, Pres./CEO
1102 Stonewall Jackson
Nashville, TN 37220
(615) 373-4502
MESBIC C *** 1,2,4,5,7,9,10,12

Valley Capital Corp.
Mr. Lamar J. Partridge, Pres.
Ms. Faye Munger
Exec. Sec./Admin. Assist.
100 W. Martin L. King Blvd., #806
Chattanooga, TN 37402
(615) 265-1557
MESBIC B *** 1,5,6,9,11,12

West Tennessee Venture Cap. Corp.
Mr. Osbie Howard, VP
Mr. Bennie L. Marshall, Mgr.
P.O. Box 300, 152 Beale St.
Memphis, TN 38101
(901) 527-6091
MESBIC B * 1,5,6,7,10,11,12

TEXAS
Branch Office
Alliance Business Investment Co.
3990 One Shell Pl.
Houston, TX 77002
(713) 224-8224
C *** 1,3,5,6,8,11,12
(Main Office in OK)

Allied Bancshares Capital Corp.
Mr. Philip A. Tuttle, Pres.
Ms. Mary Bass, Inv. Ofcr.
P.O. Box 3326
Houston, TX 77253
(713) 226-1625
D *** 1,6,8,9,11,12

Americap Corp.
Mr. James L. Hurn, Pres.
Mr. Ben Andrews, VP
One Shell Plaza, 3rd Floor
910 Louisiana
Houston, TX 77002
(713) 221-4909
C *** 1,5,6,8,12

Brittany Capital Co.
Mr. Steven S. Peden, Gen. Ptnr.
2424 LTV Tower, 1525 Elm St.
Dallas, TX 75201
(214) 954-1515
B *** 12

Business Cap. Corp. of Arlington
Mr. Keith Martin, Pres.
1112 Copeland Rd., Ste. 420
Arlington, TX 76011-4994
(817) 261-4936
A *** 12

Capital Marketing Corp.
Mr. John King Myrick, Pres.
Mr. Morris Whetstone, Gen. Mgr.
P.O. Box 1000
Keller, TX 76248
(817) 656-7380
E ** 2,9

Capital Southwest Venture Corp.
Mr. William R. Thomas, Pres.
Mr. J. Bruce Duty, VP
Mr. Patrick Hamner, Inv. Assoc.
12900 Preston Rd., Ste. 700
Dallas, TX 75230
D *** 1,3,5,6,8,9,11,12

Central Texas SBIC
Mr. David G. Hroner, Pres.
Mr. Ross Miller, Sec.
Mr. David Senior, Dir.
514 Austin Ave., P.O. Box 2600
Waco, TX 76702-2600
(817) 753-6461
A ** 5,9,12

Charter Venture Group, Inc.
Mr. Jerry Finger, Pres.
2600 Citadel Plaza Dr., 6th Fl.
Houston, TX 77008
(713) 863-0704
B *** 12

Branch Office
Citicorp Venture Capital, Ltd.
Mr. Thomas F. McWilliams, VP
Diamond Shamrock Twr., #2920-LB87
717 Harwood
Dallas, TX 75221
(214) 880-9670
E *** 12
(Main Office in NY)

Energy Capital Corp.
Mr. Herbert F. Poyner, Jr., Pres.
953 Esperson Bldg.
Houston, TX 77002
(713) 236-0006
D *** 3

Enterprise Capital Corp.
Mr. Fred S. Zeldman, Pres.
Mr. Fiore Jalarieo, Jr.
CFO/Treas.
Ms. Eta G. Paransky
Consultant/Inv. Advisor
3501 Allen Pkwy.
Houston, TX 77019
(713) 521-4401
D *** 1,5,6,7,8,12

FCA Investment Co.
Mr. R. S. Baker, Jr., Chmn.
Ms. Peggy Kliesing, Asst. Treas.
3000 Post Oak Blvd., #1790
Houston, TX 77056
(713) 965-0077
D *** 5,6,8,9,12

The Grocers SBI Corp.
Mr. Milton Levit, Pres.
3131 E. Holcombe Blvd., #101
Houston, TX 77021
(713) 747-7913
B ** 9

Branch Office
Hickory Venture Capital Corp.
3811 Turtle Creek Blvd.
#1000, LB33
Dallas, TX 75219
(214) 522-1892
E *** 12
(Main Office in AL)

InterFirst Venture Corp.
Mr. J.A. O'Donnell, Pres.
901 Main St., 10th Floor
Dallas, TX 75283
(214) 977-3164
E *** 12

Livingston Capital Ltd.
Mr. J. Livingston Kosberg, Ptnr.
Mr. Mark J. Brookner, Gen. Ptnr.
Ms. Glory S. Green, Sec.
P.O. Box 2507
Houston, TX 77252
(713) 872-3213
B *** 12

Lone Star Capital, Ltd.
Mr. Stuart Schube, Pres.
Mr. Martin D. O'Malley, Assoc.
2401 Fountainview, Ste. 950
Houston, TX 77057
(713) 266-6616
E * 1,5,6,9,12

Mapleleaf Capital Corp.
Mr. Edward M. Fink, Pres.
55 Waugh Dr., #710
Houston, TX 77007
(713) 880-4494
E *** 12

MESBIC Financial Corp. of Dallas
Mr. Thomas Gerron, VP/Controller
Mr. Don Lawhorne, Pres.
Mr. Norman Campbell, VP
12655 North Central Expwy., #814
Dallas, TX 75243
(214) 637-1597
MESBIC C *** 12

MESBIC Financial Corp. of Houston
Mr. Richard Rothfeld, Pres.
1801 Main St., Ste. 320
Houston, TX 77002
(713) 228-8321
MESBIC B * 5,8,9,10,12

Mid-State Capital Corp.
Mr. Smith E. Thomasson, Pres.
P.O. Box 7554
Waco, TX 76714
(817) 776-9500
B *** 12

MVenture Corp.
Mr. Joseph B. Longino, Jr., Pres.
Mr. J. Wayne Gaylord, Exec. VP
P.O. Box 662090
Dallas, TX 75266-2090
(214) 741-1469
D *** 1,5,6,10,11,12

Omega Capital Corp.
Mr. Ted E. Moor, Jr., Pres.
755 S. 11th St., #250
Beaumont, TX 77701
(409) 832-0221
A *** 5,12

Branch Office
Orange Nassau Capital Corp.
Mr. Richard D. Tadler, VP
One Galleria Tower
13355 Noel Rd., Ste. 635
Dallas, TX 75240
(214) 385-9685
C ** 12
(Main Office in MA)

Red River Ventures, Inc.
Mr. D.W. Morton, Pres.
777 E. 15th St.
Plano, TX 75074
(214) 422-4999
B * 12

Republic Venture Group, Inc.
Mr. Robert H. Wellborn, Pres.
Mr. William W. Richey, VP/Treas.
Mr. Bart A. McLean, Inv. Ofcr.
Ms. Sherry Richardson
Inv. Ofcr.
P.O. Box 22591
Dallas, TX 75265
(214) 922-5078
D *** 1,3,5,6,12

Retzloff Capital Corp.
Mr. James K. Hines, Pres.
Mr. Steve Retzloff, Exec. VP
Ms. Diane S. Langdon, Sec.
P.O. Box 41250
Houston, TX 77240
(713) 466-4633
C *** 5,6,9,12

San Antonio Venture Group, Inc.
Mr. Tom Woodley, Inv. Advisor
Mr. Mike Parish, Inv. Advisor
2300 W. Commerce
San Antonio, TX 79207
(512) 223-3633
B *** 4,5,6,9,10

SBI Capital Corp.
Mr. William E. Wright, Pres.
P.O. Box 771668
Houston, TX 77215-1668
(713) 975-1188
C *** 1,5,6,8

Southern Orient Capital Corp.
Dr. Cheng Ming Lee, Chmn.
2419 Fannin, Ste. 200
Houston, TX 77002
(713) 225-3369
MESBIC A * 4,9,10,12

Southwestern Ven. Cap. of TX, Inc.
Mr. James A. Bettersworth, Pres.
P.O. Box 1719
Seguin, TX 78155
(512) 379-0380
B * 12

Branch Office
Southwestern Ven. Cap. of TX, Inc.
N. Frost Ctr., Ste. 700
1250 NE Loop 410
San Antonio, TX 79209
B * 12

Sunwestern Capital Corp.
Mr. Thomas W. Wright, Pres.
Mr. James F. Leary, Exec. VP
12221 Merit Dr., #1680
Dallas, TX 75251
(214) 239-5650
C *** 1,3,5,6,8,12

Texas Capital Corp.
Mr. David Franklin, VP
Mr. Tom Beecroft, Asst. VP
1341 W. Mockingbird, #1250E
Dallas, TX 75247
(214) 638-0638
C *** 12

United Mercantile Capital Corp.
Mr. L. Joe Justice, Chmn.
P.O. Box 66
El Paso, TX 79940
(915) 533-6375
A *** 5,11

United Oriental Cap. Co.
Mr. Don J. Wang, Pres.
908 Town & Country Blvd., #310
Houston, TX 77024
(713) 461-3909
MESBIC B * 12

Wesbanc Ventures, Ltd.
Mr. Stuart Schube, Gen. Ptnr.
2401 Fountainview, #950
Houston, TX 77057
(713) 977-7421
E * 1,5,6,9,12

VIRGINIA
East West United Investment Co.
Mr. Doug Bui, Pres.
6723 Whittler Ave., Ste. 206B
McLean, VA 22101
(703) 821-6616
MESBIC A ** 4,9,12

Hillcrest Group
  James River Capital Associates
  UV Capital Corp.
Mr. A. Hugh Ewing, III
Gen. Ptnr.
Mr. James B. Farinholt, Jr.
Gen. Ptnr.
Mr. John P. Funkhouser
Gen. Ptnr.
9 S. 12th St., P.O. Box 1776
Richmond, VA 23219
(804) 643-7358
C *** 12

Metropolitan Capital Corp.
Mr. S. W. Austin, VP
2550 Huntington Ave.
Alexandria, VA 22303
(703) 960-4698
B *** 5,8

Branch Office
River Capital Corp.
1033 N. Fairfax St.
Alexandria, VA 22314
(703) 739-2100
D *** 12
(Main Office in RI)

Sovran Funding Corp.
Mr. David A. King, Jr., Pres.
Sovran Ctr., 6th Fl.
One Commercial Pl.
Norfolk, VA 23510
(804) 441-4041
C *** 12

WASHINGTON
Peoples Capital Corp.
Mr. R. W. Maider, Pres.
2411 Fourth Ave., Ste. 400
Seattle, WA 98121
(206) 344-8105
B * 1,6,9

Seafirst Capital Corp.
Mr. R. Bruce Harrod, Pres.
Columbia Seafirst Center
14th Floor
P.O. Box C-34103
Seattle, WA 98124-1103
(206) 442-3501
C * 2

WISCONSIN
Bando-McGlocklin Inv. Co., Inc.
Mr. George Schonath, CEO
Mr. Sal Bando, Pres.
Mr. Jon McGlocklin, Exec. VP
13555 Bishops Ct., Ste. 205
Brookfield, WI 53005
(414) 784-9010
C ** 5,6,9,10,11

Capital Investment, Inc.
Mr. Robert L. Banner, VP
744 N. 4th St.
Milwaukee, WI 53203
(414) 273-6560
C * 1,5,9,12

M & I Ventures Corp.
Mr. Daniel P. Howell, VP
770 N. Water St.
Milwaukee, WI 53202
(414) 765-7910
C *** 5,6,8,12

Madison Capital Corp.
Mr. Roger H. Ganser, Pres.
102 State St.
Madison, WI 53703
(608) 256-8185
B * 6,8,12

Marine Venture Capital, Inc.
Mr. H. Wayne Foreman, Pres.
Mr. Reed R. Prior, VP
111 E. Wisconsin Ave.
Milwaukee, WI 53202
(414) 765-2274
C *** 12

Branch Office
MorAmerica Capital Corp.
Mr. Steven J. Massey, VP
600 E. Mason St.
Milwaukee, WI 53202
(414) 276-3839
D *** 12
(Main Office in Iowa)

SC Opportunities, Inc.
Mr. Robert L. Ableman, VP/Sec.
Mr. Richard E. Becker, Asst. Sec.
1112 7th Ave.
Monroe, WI 53566
(608) 328-8540
MESBIC A *** 9

Super Market Investors, Inc.
Mr. John W. Andorfer, Pres.
Mr. David Maass, VP
P.O. Box 473
Milwaukee, WI 53201
(414) 547-7999
A ** 9

Twin Ports Capital Co.
Mr. Paul Leonidas, Pres.
R. F. Joki, Sec./Treas.
1230 Poplar Ave.
P.O. Box 849
Superior, WI 54880
(715) 392-5525
A * 12

Wisconsin Community Capital Inc.
Mr. Louis Fortis, Pres.
Ms. Nancy Bornstein, VP
14 W. Mifflin St., #314
Madison, WI 53703
(608) 256-3441
A * 3,5,10

Wisconsin MESBIC, Inc. (The)
Mr. Charles A. McKinney, Chmn.
Mr. William P. Beckett, Pres.
622 N. Water St., Ste. 500
Milwaukee, WI 53202
(414) 278-0377
MESBIC B *** 12

WYOMING

Capital Corp. of Wyoming, Inc.
Mr. Larry J. McDonald, Pres.
Mr. Scott Weaver, VP
Ms. Luella Brown, VP
Ms. Jean Hughley, Asst. VP
P.O. Box 3599
Casper, WY 82602
(307) 234-5438
B * 3,5,9,10,11,12

NON-SBIC MEMBERS

Mr. Robert B. Leisy
Consultant
14408 E. Whittler Blvd., B-5
P.O. Box 4405
Whittler, CA 90605
(213) 698-4862

Accel Partners
Mr. James R. Swartz, Mng. Ptnr.
Mr. Dixon R. Doll, Mg. Ptnr.
Mr. Arthur Patterson, Mng. Ptnr.
One Palmer Sq.
Princeton, NJ 08542
(609) 683-4500
E * 1,5,6,8,9,10,12

Alimansky Venture Group, Inc.
Mr. Burt Alimansky, Mng. Dir.
790 Madison Ave., Ste. 705
New York, NY 10021
(212) 472-0502
E *** 1,3,5,6,7,8,9,10,11,12

R.W. Allsop & Associates
Mr. Robert W. Allsop, Gen. Ptnr.
Mr. Gregory B. Bultman, Gen. Ptnr.
Mr. Robert L. Kuk, Gen. Ptnr.
Mr. Larry C. Maddox, Gen. Ptnr.
Mr. Paul D. Rhines, Gen. Ptnr.
2750 First Ave., NE, Ste. 210
Cedar Rapids, IA 52402
(319) 363-8971
D *** 1,5,6,9,12

Allstate Insurance Co.
    Venture Capital Division
Mr. Leonard A. Batterson
Sr. Inv. Mgr.
Allstate Plaza E-2
Northbrook, IL 60062
(312) 291-5681
E *** 1,4,5,6,8,10,11,12

Arete Ventures, Inc.
Mr. Robert W. Shaw, Jr., Pres.
5995 Barfield Rd., #220
Atlanta, GA 30328
(404) 257-9548

Arthur Andersen & Co.
Mr. John Cherin, Mng. Ptnr.
8251 Greensboro Dr., #400
McLean, VA 22102
(703) 734-7300

Arthur Andersen & Co.
Mr. Brian P. Murphy, Ptnr.
111 SW Columbia, #1400
Portland, OR 97201
(503) 220-6068

Arthur Anderson & Co.
Mr. Robert W. Philip, Ptnr.
P.O. Box 650026
Dallas, TX 75265
(214) 741-8300

Arthur Andersen & Co.
Mr. Richard J. Strotman, Ptnr.
33 W. Monroe St.
Chicago, IL 60603
(312) 580-0033

Atlantic Venture Partners
Mr. Robert H. Pratt, Gen. Ptnr.
P.O. Box 1493
Richmond, VA 23212
(804) 644-5496
D *** 12

The Babcock Group
Mr. Warner King Babcock, Pres.
Mr. Piers Curry, Baystreet Ptnrs.
P.O. Box 1022
49 Locust Ave.
New Canaan, CT 06840
(203) 972-3579

Bain Capital
Mr. Geoffrey S. Rehnert
Sr. Associate
Two Copley Pl.
Boston, MA 02116
(617) 572-3000
C *** 12

Baker & Kirk, P.C.
Mr. Michael A. Baker, Pres.
1020 Holcombe, Suite 1444
Houston, TX 77030
(713) 790-9316

Battery Ventures
Mr. Richard D. Frisble
Gen. Ptnr.
Mr. Robert G. Barrett
Gen. Ptnr.
Mr. Oliver D. Curme
Assoc.
Mr. Sheryl E. Cuker
Research Assoc.
60 Batterymarch St., $1400
Boston, MA 02110
(617) 542-0100
D *** 1

Beacon Partners
Mr. Leonard Vignola, Jr.
Mng. Ptnr.
71 Strawberry Hill Ave., #614
Stamford, CT 06902
(203) 348-8858
D *** 1,4,5,6,7,9,11

Berry Cash Southwest Ptnrship.
Mr. Harvey B Cash, Gen. Ptnr.
Mr. Glenn A. Norem, Gen. Ptrn.
Ms. Nancy J. Schuele, Assoc.
1 Galleria Tower, Ste. 1375
13355 Noel Rd.
Dallas, TX 75240
(214) 392-7279
D *** 1,8

William Blair Venture Partners
Mr. Samuel B. Guren, Gen. Ptnr.
135 S. LaSalle St., 29th Floor
Chicago, IL 60603
(312) 236-1600
E *** 12

Brownstein, Zeidman & Schomer
Mr. Thomas C. Evans, Ptnr.
1401 New York Ave., N.W., #900
Washington, DC 20036
(202) 789-5760

Burton & Co., Inc.
Mr. Reginald C. Burton, Pres.
P.O. Box 7319
Philadelphia, PA 19101-7319
(312) 263-6663

Camperdown Ventures
Mr. S. Cary Beckwith, III
Gen. Ptnr.
115 E. Camperdown Way
Greenville, SC 29601
(803) 233-7770

Capital Services & Resources, Inc.
Mr. Charles Y. Bancroft, Treas.
5159 Wheelis Dr., Ste. 104
Memphis, TN 38117
(901) 761-2156
E * 1,4,5,6,8,9

Cardinal Development Cap. Fund I
Mr. Richard F. Bannon, Ptnr.
155 E. Broad St.
Columbus, OH 43215
(614) 464-5550
E *** 1,5,6,8,9,10,11,12

Centennial Fund, The
Mr. G. Jackson Tankersley
Gen. Ptnr.
Mr. Steven C. Halstedt
Gen. Ptnr.
Mr. Charles T. Closson
Gen. Ptnr.
Mr. Mark Dubovoy
VP/Gen. Ptnr.
1999 Broadway, Suite 2100
P.O. Box 13977
Denver, CO 80202
(303) 298-9066
D *** 1,6,8

Cherry Tree Ventures
Mr. Gordon Stofer, Gen. Ptnr.
Mr. Tony Christianson, Gen. Ptnr.
Mr. Thomas Jackson, Inv. Ofcr.
Mr. John Bergstrom, Inv. Analyst
640 Northland Executive Ctr.
3600 W. 80th St.
Minneapolis, MN 55431
(612) 893-9012
D *** 1,5,6,10

Mr. Roger B. Collins
R & C Investments
P.O. Box 52586
Tulsa, OK 74152
(918) 744-5604
B * 1,3,4,5,9,10,11,12

Columbine Venture Mgmt., Inc.
Mr. Mark Kimmel, Pres.
5613 DTC Pkwy., #510
Englewood, CO 80111
(303) 694-3222

Cooley Godward Castro Hudles & Tatum
Mr. James C. Gaither, Gen. Ptnr.
One Maritime Plaza, 20th Floor
San Francisco, CA 94111
(415) 981-5252

Coopers & Lybrand
Mr. Robert H. Stavers
One Almaden Blvd., #500
San Jose, CA 95113
(408) 295-1020
1,2,3,5,6,8,9

Corp. For Innovation Development
Mr. Marion C. Dietrich, Pres/CEO
Mr. Donald K. Taylor, VP
Mr. M. Archie Leslie, VP
One N. Capitol Ave., Ste. 520
Indianapolis, IN 46204
(317) 635-7325
C *** 1,5,6,8,9

Criterion Venture Partners
Mr. David Wicks, Jr., Sr. Ptnr.
Mr. M. Scott Albert, Ptnr.
Mr. C. W. Brown, Assoc.
333 Clay St., Ste. 4300
Houston, TX 77002
(713) 751-2400
D *** 1,6,8,9,10,11,12

Dana Venture Capital Corp.
Mr. Gene C. Swartz, Pres.
P.O. Box 1000
Toledo, OH 43697
(419) 535-4780
E * 12

Deloitte Haskins & Sells
Mr. Sanford Antignas
Sr. Consultant
1114 Ave. of Americas
New York, NY 10036
(212) 790-0539

DeSoto Capital Corp.
Mr. William Rudner, Chmn.
Mr. Rudolph H. Holmes, III, Pres.
Mr. James A. Baker, Exec. VP
60 N. Third St.
Memphis, TN 38103
(901) 523-6894
A *** 5,12

Development Corp. of Montana
Mr. Richard L. Bourke, Pres.
350 N. Last Chance Gulch
P.O. Box 916
Helena, MT 59624
(406) 442-3850
B *** 12

Development Finance Corp.
of New Zealand
Mr. Chris C. Ellison, Mgr.
Mr. Andrew Stedman
Technology & Invest. Consultant
100 Spear St., Ste. 1430
San Francisco, CA 94105
(415) 777-2847

DnC Capital Corp.
Mr. Jack A. Prizzi, VP
600 Fifth Ave.
New York, NY 10020
(212) 765-4800
C *** 1,5,6,8,12

Early Stages Co. (The)
Mr. Frank W. Kuehn, Ptnr.
Mr. William Lanphear, IV, Ptnr.
Mr. Micheline L. Chau, Assoc.
244 California St., Ste. 300
San Francisco, CA 94111
(415) 986-5700
C *** 6,7,9,10

El Dorado Ventures
Mr. Brent Rider, Ptnr.
Mr. Gary Kalbach, Ptnr.
Mr. Greg S. Anderson, Gen. Mgr.
2 N. Lake Ave., Ste. 480
Pasadena, CA 91101
(818) 793-1936
D * 12

Elf Technologies, Inc.
Mr. John H. Mahar, Exec. VP
Ms. Christine Civiale, Asst. VP
High Ridge Park, P.O. Box 10037
Stamford, CT 06904
(203) 358-5120
E *** 3,5,8

Ernst & Whinney
Mr. Larry Gray, Ptnr.
5941 Variel
Woodland Hills, CA 91367
(818) 888-0707

Fine & Ambrogne
Mr. Arnold M. Zaff, Ptnr.
Exchange Place
Boston, MA 02109
(617) 367-0100

First Chicago Investment Advisors
Mr. Patrick A. McGivney, VP
Mr. T. Bondurant French, VP
Mr. Michael I. Gallie, VP
Mr. David S. Timson, VP
Three First National Plaza
Ste. 0140, 9th Fl.
Chicago, IL 60670
(312) 732-4919
D *** 1,5,6,8,9

Fostin Capital Corp.
Mr. William F. Woods, Pres.
Mr. Thomas M. Levine, Exec. VP
P.O. Box 67
Pittsburgh, PA 15230
(412) 928-8900
C *** 1,6,8

Gatti Tomerlin & Martin Corp.
Mr. John Gatti, Chmn.
Mr. Monte Tomerlin, Pres.
Mr. Harlon Martin, Jr., Exec. VP
405 N. St. Mary's, Suite 222
San Antonio, TX 78205
(512) 229-9028
E *** 1,3,5,6,9,10,12

General Electric Ven. Cap. Corp.
Mr. Harry T. Rein, Pres.
Mr. Stephen L. Waechter
VP/Treas.
3135 Easton Tnpk.
Fairfield, CT 06431
(203) 373-3356
D *** 1,5,6,8,10,12

Golder, Thoma & Cressey
Mr. Stanley C. Golder, Gen. Ptnr.
Mr. Carl D. Thoma, Gen. Ptnr.
Mr. Bryan C. Cressey, Gen. Ptnr.
Mr. Bruce V. Rauner, Gen. Ptnr.
120 S. LaSalle St., Ste. 630
Chicago, IL 60603
(312) 853-3322
E *** 1,4,5,6,8,10,11

Grayrock Capital, Ltd.
Mr. W. J. Gluck, Pres.
2 International Blvd.
Rexdale, Ont. M9W 1A2, Canada
(416) 675-4808
D *** 1,6,7,9,10

Great American Investment Corp.
Mr. James A. Arias, Pres.
Mr. Tim Scanlon, VP
4209 San Mateo NE
Albuquerque, NM 87110
(505) 883-6273
C *** 12

HLPM, Inc.
Mr. Robert W. Fletcher, Pres.
Mr. Albert L. Earley, VP
545 S. Third St.
Louisville, KY 40202
(502) 588-8459

Heizer Corp.
Mr. E.F. Heizer, Jr., Chmn./Pres.
261 S. Bluffs Edge Dr.
Lake Forest, IL 60045
(312) 641-2200

Heller Financial Inc.
Mr. Robert Spitalnio, Sr. VP
101 Park Ave.
New York, NY 10178
(212) 880-7062
E *** 5,9,10,12

Helms, Mulliss & Johnston
B. Bernard Burns, Jr., Esq.
227 N. Tryon St., P.O. Box 31247
Charlotte, NC 28231
(704) 372-9510

Houston Venture Partners
Mr. Howard Hill, Jr., Gen. Ptnr.
Mr. Thomas Fatjo, Jr., Gen. Ptnr.
Mr. Roger Ramsey, Gen. Ptnr.
Mr. Kent Smith, Gen. Ptnr.
401 S. Louisiana
Houston, TX 77002
(713) 222-8600
E * 12

Hunton & Williams
C. Porter Vaughan, III, Esq.
P.O. Box 1535
Richmond, VA 23212
(804) 788-8200

Hutton Venture Investment Ptnrs.
Mr. James E. McGrath, Pres.
1 Battery Park Plaza, #1801
New York, NY 10004
(212) 742-6486
D *** 1,5,6,8

IEG Venture Mgmt., Inc.
Mr. Francis I. Blair, Pres.
Mrs. Marian M. Zamlynski
Op. Mgr./VP
401 N. Michigan Ave., #2020
Chicago, IL 60611
(312) 644-0890
C *** 1,3,6,8

Indiana Capital Corp.
Mr. Samuel Rea, Pres.
5612 Jefferson Blvd., W.
Ft. Wayne, IN 46804
(219) 432-8622

Inst. of Private Enterprise
Dr. Rollie Tillman, Dir.
312 Carroll Hall, #012-A
Chapel Hill, NC 27514
(919) 962-8201

Interstate Capital Corp.
Mr. William C. McConnell Jr. Pres.
701 E. Camino Real, #9A
Boca Raton, FL 33432
(305) 395-8466
B *** 3,5,6,8

Investors in Industry
(See 31 under T)

Japan Associate Finance Co., Ltd.
Mr. Teiji Imahara, Chmn.
Toshiba Bldg., 10th Fl.
1-1-1 Shibaura Minato-KU
Tokyo, Japan
(03) 456-5101
E *** 1,5,9,10

Jenkins Huchison & Gilchrist
Mr. John R. Holzgraefe, Ptnr.
Mr. Mark Wigder, Ptnr.
Mr. W. Alan Kailer, Ptnr.
1455 Ross Ave., 29th Flr.
Dallas, TX 75202
(214) 855-4500

Kirkland & Ellis
Mr. Edward T. Swan
200 E. Randolph Dr.
Chicago, IL 60601
(312) 861-2465

Kieinwort, Benson (NA) Corp.
Mr. Alan L. J. Bowen, Sr., VP
Mr. Christopher Wright, VP
Ms. Michele Hurtubise
Office Mgr.
333 S. Grand, #2900
Los Angeles, CA 90071
(213) 680-2297
E * 3,5,6,9,11,12

Knight & Irish Associates, Inc.
Dr. Joan S. Irish, Pres.
Ms. Faith I. Bliga, VP
420 Lexington Ave., Ste. 2358
New York, NY 10170
(212) 490-0135

Lord, Bissell & Brook
Mr. John K. O'Connor, Ptnr.
115 S. LaSalle St., #3500
Chicago, IL 60603
(312) 443-0615

Lubrizol Enterprises, Inc.
Mr. Donald L. Murfin, Pres.
Mr. Bruce H. Grasser, VP
Mr. James R. Glynn, VP-Fin./Treas.
Mr. David R. Anderson, VP
29400 Lakeland Blvd.
Wickliffe, OH 44092
(216) 943-4200
E *** 8

MRI Ventures
Mr. Charles Moll, VP
Ms. Carol Radosevich, Ven. Mgr.
1650 University Blvd., NE, #500
Albuquerque, NM 87102
(505) 768-6200
D *** 1,5,6,8,12

Madison Venture Capital Corp.
Mr. Norman C. Schultz, Pres.
26515 Carmel Rancho Blvd., #201
Carmel, CA 93923
(408) 625-9650

Manuf. Hanover Vent. Cap. Corp.
Mr. Thomas J. Sandleithner, Pres.
Mr. Edward L. Koch, III, VP
140 E. 45th St., 30th Fl.
New York, NY 10017
(212) 350-6701
E *** 1,4,5,6,7,9,10,11,12

Mayer, Brown, & Platt
Herbert B. Max, Esq.
520 Madison Ave.
New York, NY 10022
(212) 437-7132

Med-Wick Associates, Inc.
Mr. A.A.T. Wickersham, Chmn./Pres.
1902 Fleet National Bank Bldg.
Providence, RI 02903
(401) 751-5270

Menlo Ventures
Mr. Ken E. Joy, Gen. Ptnr.
3000 Sand Hill Rd.
Menlo Park, CA 94025
(415) 854-8540
E *** 12

Michigan Inv. Div., Treas. Dept.
Mr. Michael J. Finn, Admin.
P.O. Box 15128
Lansing, MI 48901
(517) 373-4330
D * 12

Miller Venture Partners
Mr. William I. Miller
Gen. Ptnr.
Mr. Ira G. Peppercorn
Sr. Inv. Mgr.
P.O. Box 808
Columbus, IN 47202
(812) 376-3331
B *** 3,5,6,8,11

Moore Berson Lifflander & Mewhinney
Mr. Joel L. Berson
595 Madison Ave.
New York, NY 10022

Morgan Holland Ventures Corp.
Mr. James F. Morgan, Mng. Ptnr.
Mr. Daniel J. Holland, Mng. Ptnr.
Mr. John A. Delahanty, Gen. Ptnr.
Mr. Robert Rosbe, Jr., Gen. Ptnr.
Mr. Edwin M. Kania, Jr., Assoc.
1 Liberty Sq.
Boston, MA 02109
(617) 423-1765
E *** 1,5,6,8

Morgenthaler Ventures
Mr. David T. Morgenthaler
Mng. Ptnr.
Mr. Robert D. Pavey
Gen. Ptnr.
Mr. Paul S. Brentlinger
Gen. Ptnr.
Mr. Robert C. Bellas, Jr.
Gen. Ptnr.
700 National City Bank Bldg.
Cleveland, OH 44114
(216) 621-3070
E *** 1,5,6,8,10

Morrison & Foerster
Tino Kamarck, Esq.
Marco Adelfrio, Esq.
200 Pennsylvania Ave., NW
Washington, DC 20006
(202) 887-1500

NEPA Venture Fund, L.P.
Mr. Frederick J. Beste, III, Pres.
Ben Franklin Adv. Tech. Ctr.
Lehigh Univ.
Bethlehem, PA 18015
(215) 865-6550
E *** 12

New Enterprise Associates
Mr. Charles Newhall III,
Gen. Ptnr.
300 Cathedral St., Ste. 110
Baltimore, MD 21201
(301) 244-0115
E * 1,6

Nippon Investment & Finance Co. Ltd.
Mr. Yasutoshi Sasada, Pres.
Mr. Motoki Sugiyama, Gen. Mgr.
39F, Nishi-Shinjuku 1-25-1,
Shinjuku-ku
Tokyo 163 JAPAN
(03) 349-0961
E *** 12

NBM Participatie Beheer B.V.
Mr. Michiel A. de Haan, Gen. Mgr.
Postbus 1800
1000 BV AMSTERDAM
The Netherlands, NL
(020) 543-3346
E * 1,5,6,8,10,11

Noro-Moseley Partners
Mr. Charles Moseley, Gen. Ptnr.
100 Galleria Pkwy., #1240
Atlanta, GA 30339
(404) 955-0020

North American Capital Corp.
Mr. Stanley P. Roth, Chmn.
510 Broad Hollow Rd., #205
Melville, NY 11747
(516) 752-9696
E * 12

North American Cap. Group, Ltd.
Mr. Gregory I. Kravitt, Pres.
Ms. Mindy Warshawsky, Assoc.
7250 W. Cicero
Lincolnwood, IL 60646
(312) 982-1010
D *** 2,4,5,6,9,10

Olwine, Connelly, Chase, et al
Mr. Roger Mulvihill
299 Park Ave.
New York, NY 10017
(212) 207-1831

Onondaga Vent. Capital Fund, Inc.
Mr. Irving W. Schwartz, Exec. VP
327 State Tower Bldg.
Syracuse, NY 13202
(315) 478-0157
B *** 12

Oxford Partners
Mr. Kenneth Rind, Gen. Ptnr.
1266 Main St.
Stamford, CT 06902
(203) 964-0592
E *** 1,6,8

Ozanam Capital Co.-I, LP
Ms. Janis L. Mullin, Gen. Ptnr.
Mr. Adam Robins, Gen., Ptnr.
Mr. Robert Berliner, Gen. Ptnr.
4711 Golf Rd., #706
Skokie, IL 60076
(312) 674-2297
B *** 5,9

Pathfinder Venture Cap. Fund
Mr. A.J. Greenshields, Gen. Ptnr.
7300 Metro Blvd., Ste. 585
Minneapolis, MN 55435
(612) 835-1121
D *** 1,5,6,8

Peat, Marwick, Mitchell & Co.
Mr. Terence D. Dibble, Ptnr.
725 South Figueroa St.
Los Angeles, CA 90017
(213) 972-4000

Peat, Marwick, Mitchell & Co.
Mr. Ronald R. Booth, Ptnr.
1700 IDS Center
Minneapolis, MN 55402
(612) 341-2222

Peat, Marwick, Mitchell & Co.
Mr. Michael E. Lavin, Ptnr.
303 E. Wacker Dr.
Chicago, IL 60601
(312) 938-5043

Peat, Marwick, Mitchell & Co.
Mr. Edgar R. Wood, Jr., Ptnr.
1800 First Union Pl.
Charlotte, NC 28282
(704) 335-5300

Pepper, Hamilton & Scheetz
Mr. Michael B. Staebler, Ptnr.
Mr. Hugh D. Camitta, Esq.
100 Renaissance Ctr., Ste. 3600
Detroit, MI 48243
(313) 259-7110

Peregrine Associates
Mr. Gene I. Miller, Ptnr.
Mr. Frank LaHaye, Ptnr.
606 Wilshire Blvd., Ste. 602
Santa Monica, CA 90401
(213) 458-1441
E *** 1,5,6,8,9,10,12

Pioneer Capital Corp.
Mr. Christopher W. Lynch, Ptnr.
Mr. Frank M. Polestra, Ptnr.
60 State St.
Boston, MA 02109
(617) 742-7825
D * 12

Piper, Jaffray & Hopwood, Inc.
Mr. Frank Bennett,
Mr. R. Hunt Greene, 1st VP
Piper Jaffray Tower
222 So. 9th St.
P.O. Box 28
Minneapolis, MN 55402
(612) 342-6000
D *** 1,5,6,8,9,10

Branch Office
Piper, Jaffray & Hopwood
Mr. Gary L. Takacs, VP
1600 IBM Building
Seattle, WA 98101
D *** 1,5,6,8,9,10

Primus Capital Fund
Mr. Loyal Wilson, Mng. Ptnr.
Mr. David A. DeVore, Ptnr.
Mr. William C. Mulligan, Ptnr.
One Cleveland Ctr., #2140
Cleveland, OH 44114
(216) 621-2185
E *** 1,5,6,8,9,12

RBK Management Co.
Mr. Robert B. Kaplan, Pres.
140 S. Dearborn St., #420
Chicago, IL 60603
(312) 263-6058

Reprise Capital Corp.
Mr. Stanley Tulchin, Chmn.
Mr. Irwin B. Nelson, Pres.
591 Stewart Ave.
Garden City, NY 11530
(516) 222-1028
E *** 12

Riordan & McKinzie
Michael P. Ridley, Esq.
300 South Grand Ave., Ste. 2900
Los Angeles, CA 90017
(213) 629-4824

Rothschild Ventures, Inc.
Mr. Jess L. Belser, Pres.
One Rockefeller Pl.
New York, NY 10020
(212) 757-6000
E *** 1,5,6,8,12

Rust Capital Ltd.
Mr. Jeffrey C. Garvey, Pres.
Mr. Kenneth P. DeAngelis, Exec. VP
Mr. Joseph C. Aragona, VP
Mr. William P. Wood, VP
114 W. 7th St., 1300 Norwood Twr.
Austin, TX 78701
(512) 479-0055
D **** 1,4,5,6,12

Salomon Brothers, Inc.
Mr. Melvin W. Ellis, VP
One New York Plaza
New York, NY 10004
(212) 747-6293
E * 1,6,8

Santa Fe Private Equity Fund
Mr. A. David Silver, Gen. Ptnr.
Ms. Kay Tsunemori, Assoc.
Mr. Kyle A. Legkoff, Assoc.
Ms. Angela H. Peck, Assoc.
524 Camino Del Monte Sol
Santa Fe, NM 87501
(505) 983-1769
D *** 6

SB Capital Corp., Ltd.
Mr. Mitch Kostuch, Exec. VP
Mr. Peter Standeven, VP
Mr. David McCart, Inv. Ofcr.
85 Bloor St., E., #506
Toronto, Ontario M4W 1A9
(416) 967-5439
D *** 1,5,6,8,12

Scientific Advances, Inc.
Mr. Charles G. James, Pres.
Mr. Paul F. Purcell, VP
Mr. Thomas W. Harvey, VP
Mr. Daniel J. Shea, VP
601 W. Fifth Ave.
Columbus, OH 43201
(614) 294-5541
D *** 8

Security Pacific Bus. Credit, Inc.
Mr. Nicholas Battaglino, VP
Mr. David J. Freidman, VP
228 E. 45th St.
New York, NY 10017
(212) 309-9302
E ** 5,9,12

South Atlantic Venture Fund
Mr. Donald Burton, Gen. Ptnr.
Mr. Richard Brandewie, Gen. Ptnr.
Ms. Sandra Barber, Admin. Ptnr.
220 East Madison, Suite 530
Tampa, FL 33602-4825
(813) 229-7400
D *** 1,5,6,8,10,12

Spensley, Horn, Jubas & Lubitz
Mr. Bruce W. McRoy, Esq., Ptnr.
1880 Century Park E., #500
Los Angeles, CA 90067
(213) 553-5050

Stephenson Merchant Banking
Mr. A. Emmet Stephenson, Jr.
Sr. Ptnr.
Mr. Thomas Kent Mitchell
Director
100 Garfield St.
Denver, CO 80206
(303) 355-6000
E *** 1,5,6,9,10,11,12

S.W.S. Ltd.
Mr. Steven B. Schaffel, Pres.
Mr. Ira B. Raymond, Exec. VP
Mr. Wendell H. Jones, VP
122 E. 42nd St.
New York, NY 10168
(212) 682-9550
E * 4,11,12

31 Capital Corp.
Mr. David R. Shaw, Pres.
Ms. Dorothy Langer
99 High St., Ste. 1530
Boston, MA 02110
(617) 542-8560

Taylor International
Mr. Don Snow
1801 Quincy St., N.W.
Washington, D.C. 20011
(202) 955-1330

Taylor & Turner
Mr. Marshall Turner, Gen. Ptnr.
Mr. William Taylor, Gen. Ptnr.
220 Montgomery St., Penthouse 10
San Francisco, CA 94104
(415) 398-6821
D * 1,5,6,8

Tektronix Development Co.
Mr. M.H. Chaffin, Jr.
VP/Gen. Mgr.
P.O. Box 4600-M/S 94-383
Beaverton, OR 97075
(503) 629-1121

Texas Infinity Corp.
Mr. C. Charles Bahr, CEO
P.O. Box 2678
Richardson, TX 75083
(214) 231-7070

Tulsa Industrial Authority
Mr. Rick L. Weddle, Gen. Mgr.
616 S. Boston
Tulsa, OK 74119
(918) 585-1201
E *** 5,6

UNC Ventures
Mr. Edward Dugger, III, Pres.
Mr. James W. Norton, Jr., VP
195 State St., #700
Boston, MA 02109
(617) 723-8300
E *** 1,5,6,8,11

Venad Management, Inc.
Ms. Joy London, Ptnr.
375 Park Ave., #3303
New York, NY 10152
(212) 759-2800

Venco SBIC
Bill McAleir, Chmn.
Phil Bardos, Pres.
One Financial Square
Oxnard, CA 93030
(805) 656-4621
B * 5,6,12

The Venture Capital Fund
  of New England
Mr. Richard Farrell, Gen. Ptnr.
100 Franklin St.
Boston, MA 02110
(617) 451-2575
C *** 1,5,8

Venture Economics, Inc.
Mr. Stanley Pratt, Chmn.
Ms. Jane K. Morris, VP
16 Laurel Ave., P.O. Box 348
Wellesley Hills, MA 02181
(617) 431-8100

Venture Founders Corp.
Mr. Alexander Dinges, Jr., Pres.
Mr. Grogory Hulecki, Inv. Mgr.
Mr. Ross Yelter, Treas.
One Cranberry Hill
Lexington, MA 02173
(617) 863-0900
D *** 1,5,6,8

Whitehead Associates, Inc.
Mr. Joseph A. Orlando, Pres.
Mr. William E. Engbers, VP
15 Valley Dr.
Greenwich, CT 06830
(203) 629-4633
D *** 1,5,6,8,10,12

William Blair Venture Partners
Mr. Samuel B. Guren
Gen. Ptnr.
Mr. Scott F. Meadow
Gen. Ptnr.
Mr. James Crawford, III
Gen. Ptnr.
Mr. Gregg S. Newmark, Assoc.
135 S. LaSalle St., 29th Fl.
Chicago, IL 60603
(312) 236-1600
E *** 12

10

THE NATIONAL VENTURE CAPITAL ASSOCIATION

The National Venture Capital Association (NVCA) is open by invitation to all venture capital organizations, corporate financiers and individual venture capitalists who are responsible for investing private capital in young companies on a professional basis.

Many NVCA members do *not* finance start-up companies but will consider funding once the company has gotten off the ground; many, however, *will* consider investments in start-up companies.

From the new entrepreneur's perspective, the NVCA's most useful service is its Annual Directory — *which it will make available to you at no charge.* It is an uncommonly clear and well-organized publication which should be in every new entrepreneur's library.

You will have to send the NVCA a self-addressed No. 10 business envelope with the correct amount of postage affixed. As we write this, postal rates are 22¢ for the first ounce and 17¢ for each additional ounce. The directory weighs eight ounces; therefore, your return envelope must carry postage in the amount of $1.41.

Send your request to:

National Venture Capital Association
1655 North Fort Myer Drive, Suite 700
Arlington, VA 22209

VCN: VENTURE CAPITAL NETWORK

We are familiar with VCN — Venture Capital Network — and yet we still find ourselves occasionally referring to it as Venture *Computer* Network.

The mistake, I suppose, is understandable since VCN is really a computerized information "matching" service for entrepreneurs and investors.

VCN is, in fact, a wonderful new opportunity for start-up entrepreneurs. Yet relatively few entrepreneurs are aware of its existence and availability. The purpose of this chapter is to introduce you to VCN and to enable you to take advantage of its unique resources.

What is VCN?

Venture Capital Network, Inc. is a not-for-profit corporation managed by the Office of Small Business Programs of the University of New Hampshire. VCN's essential purpose is to introduce entrepreneurs to individual venture investors and to venture capital firms interested in early-stage financing.

Which entrepreneurs are most likely to benefit from participation in VCN?

Those who require between $50,000 and $750,000 of equity-type financing.

Who are the VCN investors?

They represent a virtually invisible segment of the venture capital markets. They are a diverse and diffuse population of individuals of means, many of whom have created their own successful ventures. They look for products and services in markets with significant growth potential and require rewards commensurate with the risks they take.

VCN investors are required to certify that they are accredited investors as defined in Rule 501 of the SEC's Regulation D (Rules Governing the Limited Offer and Sale of Securities Under the Securities Act of 1933) or that they have such knowledge and experience in financial and business matters that they are capable of evaluating the merits and risks of prospective investments, as specified in Rule 506 of Regulation D.

How does VCN work?

VCN maintains a confidential data base of Investment Opportunity Profiles submitted by entrepreneurs and a confidential data base of Investment Interest Profiles submitted by investors.

Using a two-stage process, VCN submits to investors those investment opportunities that meet their screening criteria. Both parties remain anonymous throughout this process.

At the conclusion of the process, entrepreneurs are introduced to those investors interested in pursuing an investment opportunity.

VCN can provide no assurance that particular entrepreneurs will be matched with any prospective investors.

VCN maintains a record of the reasons investors reject investment opportunities. This information is reported to VCN entrepreneurs.

VCN's role terminates with the introduction of entrepreneurs and investors.

What does VCN charge for this service?

Presently, a fee of $100 is charged for each Investment Opportunity Profile submitted by an entrepreneur. This fee provides VCN service for a six-month period.

VCN receives no fees, commissions, or other remuneration related to the eventual outcome of entrepreneur/investor introductions.

Does VCN evaluate applications?

No. VCN is neither an investment advisor nor a broker-dealer of securities. VCN provides only an information service for entrepreneurs and investors.

VCN neither evaluates nor endorses the merits of investment opportunities presented through its services. VCN conducts no investigations to verify either the accuracy or completeness of information provided by entrepreneurs and investors.

Where can an entrepreneur secure additional information and a registration form?

By writing or calling:

Venture Capital Network, Inc.
Post Office Box 882
Durham, NH 03824
(603) 862-3556

12

CORPORATE INVESTORS

Some of America's largest and most familiar companies are also in the venture capital business. They tend to keep a "low profile" with regard to their activities in this area — typically known only to venture capital colleagues — but they are a potential resource for new entrepreneurs (particularly if their product or service is related to the company's business).

Venture Capital Affiliates of 5 Major Corporations

1. **Caterpillar Venture Capital, Inc.**
   100 N.E. Adams Street, Peoria, IL 61629
   (309) 675-5503
   Contacts: Jack W. Dennis, William B. Heming, Robert L. Powers.

2. **General Electric Venture Capital Corporation**
   3135 Easton Turnpike, Fairfield, CT 06431
   (203) 373-3333
   Contacts: Harry T. Rein, Stephen L. Waechter.

3. Hewlett-Packard Company Corporate Investments
3000 Hanover Street, Palo Alto, CA 94304
(415) 857-7308
Contacts: Robert Greeley, Elizabeth Obershaw.

4. Tenneco Ventures, Inc.
1010 Milam, Suite T2919, Houston, TX 77001
(713) 757-8776
Contacts: James J. Kowlowski, Carl S. Stutts, Richard L. Wambold.

5. Xerox Venture Capital
800 Long Ridge Road, Stamford, CT 06904
(203) 329-8711
Contacts: Richard J. Hayes, Sr., Lawrence R. Robinson, III.

13

YOUR CUSTOMERS AND SUPPLIERS

Most of this book (other than Chapter 2) has been directed towards the process of raising money from "outsiders," individuals and organizations who are not familiar with your business until you bring it to their attention.

This chapter will introduce you to two financing sources who are not only familiar with your business, but who are nearly as interested as you are in its growth and prosperity.

1. Your Customers

Entrepreneurs are typically so grateful for having any customers at all that they hesitate to jeopardize their relationship.

If you think about it, your customer has already taken a bit of a risk by electing to do business with a new company. That would suggest that he is confident (probably even impressed) about your product or service.

If you explain your cash flow needs to him, the chances are that he will respond favorably to your request for expedited payment.

One company worked out this payment formula with its customers:

- 40% with the order.
- 40% on delivery.
- 20% within 30 days.

None of them resisted, and their accelerated (even advance) payments helped this new business to survive during its difficult early days.

The moral of the story is: Don't overlook your customers as prospective — and effective — financing sources.

2. Your Suppliers

Making comfortable payment arrangements with your suppliers is the flip side of your cash flow dealings with your customers.

You want your customers to pay you as *quickly* as possible.

You want to pay your suppliers as *slowly* as possible.

If your suppliers like and trust you; if you have never mislead them or mistreated them; if you have kept all of the promises which you made to them, then you are in a wonderful position to secure their cooperation in extending your accounts payable over as long a time frame as they can live with.

Like your customers, they have a vested interest in your success.

14

"THE BIG 8" PLUS 2

There was a time, and it was not very long ago, when most of the nation's largest accounting firms — the so-called "Big 8" — would barely consider taking on a small, new business as a client.

The times have changed.

Today, these same firms are actively and aggressively seeking small companies as clients. They've read the statistics and they know as well as anyone that the majority of new jobs and new capital is being created by the new businesses which they so recently shunned.

This is not to say that a single practitioner accountant is not entirely appropriate for a new business. He most certainly is, and there is no reason whatsoever to seek a larger firm if you are satisfied with your present accounting arrangement.

However, if you have no particular loyalties to an accountant, you should know that these major accounting firms are now accessible even to new entrepreneurs.

These large firms have disadvantages — no matter how polite they are, you are still a very small client in a sea of corporate whales — but they also have considerable advantages for the new entrepreneur.

Perhaps most importantly, they have immense credibility within the banking and investment community — and the very fact that you are their client will reflect well on your prospects.

They also have wide experience in the preparation of business plans, and they are familiar with the documentation venture capitalists and lenders need to make positive decisions within their "comfort zone."

To encourage small businesses, many of these firms have established special departments designed to meet the needs of new entrepreneurs. They are typically headed by partners who understand the needs of new businesses, and enjoy helping them grow. If you can find such a partner within one of the leading firms, the ensuing relationship may become one of your best early entrepreneurial decisions.

Alphabetically, the so-called "Big 8" accounting firms are:

1. **Arthur Andersen & Co.**
2. **Coopers & Lybrand**
3. **Deloitte Haskins + Sells**
4. **Ernst & Whinney**
5. **Peat, Marwick, Mitchell & Co.**
6. **Price Waterhouse & Co.**
7. **Touche Ross**
8. **Arthur Young**

Two other firms are so close to the "Big 8" in size that we have included them as well: Grant Thornton International and KMG Main Hurdman.

Virtually all of these firms have offices in most every good-size city in America, and they will each send you material introducing you to their firm. Today, these firms have taken a marketing lesson from Uncle Sam: *As a promising new entrepreneur, they want you!*

You have been introduced to more than 400 specific sources of capital as well as to the fundamental financing techniques which are available to the new entrepreneur.

At this point, you are probably feeling exhausted as well as exhilarated. Exhausted because we've covered a great deal of ground; exhilarated because we've shared the discovery that it's high ground — that there *is* start-up capital "out there!"

However, despite the prevailing sense of cautious optimism, we could not conclude this book without one additional observation: *Never enter into any financing arrangements which make you uneasy or which strike you as being unreasonable. If you feel that way, you are probably right — and you should seek an alternative source. Successful entrepreneurs tend to have sound instincts!*

They also tend to have good fortune — and we wish you all the best as you begin the process of building yours!

ABOUT THE AUTHOR

Steve Kahn is an author, attorney and entrepreneur. As an entrepreneur, he has created new businesses in publishing, cable television and real estate. He has been the Executive Producer of "The Miss American Teen-Ager Pageant" for the ABC Television Network and a feature columnist for The New York Times Syndicate with a weekly audience of ten million Sunday newspaper readers. As an attorney, he served as Special Counsel and Director of Investor Relations for the Tishman Real Estate & Construction Co., Inc. He is the author of "THE SECURE EXECUTIVE: The Secret of Becoming One, Being One, Staying One." He holds a B.S. degree from New York University and a J.D. degree from New York Law School.

ABOUT THE NO NONSENSE
SUCCESS SERIES

More people than ever before are thinking about going into business for themselves — and the No Nonsense Success Guides have been created to provide useful information for this growing and ambitious audience. Look for these related No Nonsense Success Guides: *The Self-Employment Test . . . Getting Into The Mail Order Business . . . How To Run A Business Out of Your House . . . How To Own And Operate A Franchise . . . Getting Into The Consulting Business.*